Developing
Skeptical and Critical
Thinking
in
Psychology

John Marton

TRAFFORD

Printed in Victoria, Canada

A cataloguing record for this book that includes the U.S. Library of Congress Classification number, the Library of Congress Call number and the Dewey Decimal cataloguing code is available from the National Library of Canada. The complete cataloguing record can be obtained from the National Library's online database at: www.nlc-bnc.ca/amicus/index-e.html
ISBN: 1-4120-3647-X

TRAFFORD

This book was published on-demand in cooperation with Trafford Publishing. On-demand publishing is a unique process and service of making a book available for retail sale to the public taking advantage of on-demand manufacturing and Internet marketing. **On-demand publishing** includes promotions, retail sales, manufacturing, order fulfilment, accounting and collecting royalties on behalf of the author.

Suite 6E, 2333 Government St., Victoria, B.C. V8T 4P4, CANADA

Phone	250-383-6864	Toll-free	1-888-232-4444 (Canada & US)
Fax	250-383-6804	E-mail	sales@trafford.com
Web site	www.trafford.com	TRAFFORD PUBLISHING IS A DIVISION OF TRAFFORD HOLDINGS LTD.	
Trafford Catalogue #04-1475		www.trafford.com/robots/04-1475.html	

10   9   8   7   6   5   4   3   2

Acknowledgements

It would be impossible to express my deep gratitude to all those involved in making this book possible. Appreciation is due to my family for their patience, encouragement, and ideas. I would not have persevered without the wonderfully enthusiastic response of the many students who worked with earlier drafts. Finally, my thanks to David Myers, Gerald Peterson, and Jane Halonen who each provided encouragement and valuable feedback.

June 2004

North Island College

Courtenay, BC, Canada

marton@mars.ark.com

Contents

Introduction (for instructors)

Critical thinking is the ability to make judgments and draw inferences based on empirical evidence. I have found that the greatest obstacle to teaching critical thinking skills in psychology, especially in introductory courses is the illusion of knowledge. Students enter the course with life experience, pop beliefs, and smatterings of pseudoscientific information.

For development in thinking to occur, questioning, inquiry, and doubt about preexisting knowledge must take place. It is the illusion of certain knowledge that impedes the searching.

These fables are supplements to other approaches to the teaching of critical thinking skills in psychology.

The acquisition of skeptical and critical thinking skills is often considered to be one of the goals of introductory psychology instruction (Halonen, 1995). However, the achievement of these goals has been elusive.

A number of factors combine to limit easy success. Survey research indicates a significant percentage of North Americans believe in phenomena for which supportive evidence is lacking. Overall, half of Americans believe in psychic or spiritual healing, and extrasensory perception (ESP); a third or more believe in such things as haunted houses, possession by the devil, ghosts, telepathy, extraterrestrial beings having visited earth, and clairvoyance (Gallup Organization, 2001). A substantial body of psychological research demonstrates that everyday social experience is fertile soil for the growth and maintenance of these types of beliefs even in the absence of valid evidence.

These beliefs are maintained in part by the power of media representations, vivid anecdotes, and peer dynamics as well as by a variety of social cognitive errors, including illusory correlation, confirmation bias, hindsight bias, selective attention and recall, and weak understanding of probabilities (Gilovich, 1991; Shermer, 1997).

The instructor who wishes to teach skeptical and critical thinking is faced with complex issues. She may just ignore the existing context of students' paranormal beliefs and teach critical thinking in other or abstract contexts. This approach may result in little generalization of critical thinking to students' beliefs (Adler, 1991). Alternatively, the instructor may mount a frontal assault on student paranormal beliefs. However, the dissonance created by the gulf between instructor's views and existing views of the student, peers, and media may often be resolved by dismissal of the instructor' views and a distancing of the student from the methods of science.

An emphasis placed on direct debunking of myths contradicts the more general social tendency to confirm and affirm. Limited evidence does indicate that frontal assault on paranormal beliefs in the context of an abstract critical thinking course is likely to result in little long-term change (Peterson, 2001).

The unique narrative approach used in this book has demonstrated increased student engagement and satisfaction. It has also demonstrated improved critical thinking skills, especially in the area of significantly reducing students' initial high credence to claims of the paranormal (Marton, 2002).

This book consists of ten interconnected "fables". The protagonist is a young woman student. The other main character is a semi-retired eccentric female professor who mentors the younger student. Together they encounter various typical life situations, as well as some psychological puzzles. The puzzles involve phenomena such as claims of psychic powers, unidentified flying objects, confabulated memories, difficult-to-explain gender miscommunications, and so on.

The topics of the fables parallel the organization of standard introductory psychology texts. For example, the first five fables deal with critical thinking, sensation and perception, consciousness, learning, and memory.

These two characters work together, demonstrating critical thinking as well as more general attributes of psychological thinking.

The fables have been used as a supplement to standard introductory psychology texts. They promote critical thinking, application of psychological principles to normal life situations, classroom discussion, and active participation. I have often asked students to provide brief written responses to the questions posed at the end of each chapter.

This activity provides an engaging and vibrant experience that supports a deeper processing of the concepts than is provided for by more abstract and passive teaching or learning practices. Students engaging in the written responses nearly universally adopt the critical thinking perspective. From that point on, cognitive dissonance acts to support critical thinking.

Introduction (for students)

These fables are ways of drawing you into thinking carefully about psychology. They provide you with the opportunity to link theory and principles with everyday life. I have tried to show how basic psychological ideas can be applied to events and issues in life that we all encounter. The stories will test your comprehension of portions of the course. They provide you with the opportunity to be an active, creative learner. I hope you enjoy and learn!

Fables for Developing Psychological Thinking

1.

The Truly Cold Reading

I had my B.A. in psychology, but I was not sure where it could take me but I did want it to take me into a bigger world. An opportunity came when I received an e-mail from a former psychology professor. Professor Elinore, my favorite teacher, had retired and become a 'psychological detective', using her psychology skills to solve problems. She wanted companionship and help with her work in exchange for mentoring. We had agreed that I would spend some time living and working with her.

I knew from the two courses that I had taken from Professor Elinore that she was brilliant and eccentric. On our first evening she explained that since retirement from teaching she had built a consulting practice. "Mariah", she filled me in, "I solve problems in human behavior and cognition. That is why I have come to be called the 'psychological detective'. You need to understand I am not one of those psychologists who devote themselves to providing recipes for how to get along better with others. As you know, I am not tempted to raise the self-esteem of persons who do not deserve to feel good about themselves. I also do not feel a calling to tell people how to develop a better personality in three easy steps."

"What I do care about is approaching problems through two essentials: the principles of psychology and of logic. This allows me to develop strategies that eventually lead to solutions that can be of practical usefulness. Once I develop a strategy and figure out what questions need answering, I need data. I am getting too old to go out and make the observations that are the basis of all useful information. That is going to be your role. Tomorrow Professor Brown is coming over at eight. He is a Dean at the University. He has a problem for which he has asked for my help. So, I want you to sit in with Dr. Brown and me. He has a serious problem for us.

The next morning I was alone when the phone rang. It was Dr. Brown. He had a deep, confident sounding voice. "I thought it best to give you the topic which I wish to discuss tonight" he started. "There is a curious case of a 'cold reader' who has come on campus. Are you familiar with the term 'cold reader' or 'cold reading'?" I told him I was not but would look it up before our meeting.

Dr. Brown repeated what he had heard from students; "I have never met anyone in my life who has understood me so well" (from a student who had spent all of 20 minutes with the 'cold reader'); "How could he know so much about me, unless he was psychic?" "He is completely amazing." Dr. Brown's tone dripped with derision as he went on to say that he had heard one student had ended a romantic relationship based on the cold reader's advice, and another one has dropped out of college supposedly based on his readings. Dr. Brown explained that there was worry about the influence of this reader on impressionable and vulnerable students, as well as the waste of money.

I looked up the term that afternoon. The most useful site was the skeptic's dictionary <http://skepdic.com/>. It seems that 'cold reading' refers to a set of controversial techniques. The 'reading' part refers to an individual with presumed special gifts or sensitivities being able to 'read' the personality and future of the subject (the person being read). Sometimes tarot cards, crystals, examining lines on the palm, or just holding hands is used to assist the reader, in receiving messages, signals, or vibrations. The 'cold' part refers to the fact that the reader has no prior knowledge of the person who is the subject of the reading. The subject might be someone who has answered an advertisement, or has possibly heard of the reader through reputation, or may have been referred by a friend who has been 'read'.

The skeptic's dictionary indicated that believers in the idea that some gifted individuals have special powers to see into the essence of a subject's personality and future, often have powerful stories to tell. Typically these stories are personal or involve friends and relatives who were told deeply private and informative things, by a reader who had never met them before and knew nothing about them prior to the meeting. Often there are details about the future that have turned out later, sometimes decades later, to apparently come true.

As I was consulting the dictionary I recalled a story my mother liked to tell. When she was about 12 years old, a palm reader at a fair told her that she would later in life "cross a large body of water" and this would result in a big change in her life. At the age of 25, my father and she left their native Poland to immigrate to Kansas, crossing the Atlantic Ocean. It was a big change in her life. Usually a careful thinker, my mother marveled at the powers of this palm reader and told the story many times.

I bit my tongue whenever she told the story. I could have asked, how many people do not cross a large body of water sometime in their adult life? Who does not drive across a bridge, fly over an ocean, take a boat across a lake? On making the crossing, how many do not meet someone important (maybe a future wife or husband), or obtain a job, or attend a college, have children, or have something significant happen to them? My mother interpreted that the trip across the Atlantic Ocean from Poland to Kansas had been predicted 13 years in advance. That would have been truly marvelous! However, just about anything occurring later in life, even if she had never crossed an ocean could have been interpreted as the 'prediction' coming 'true'. Of course it would be unkind and no fun to point this out to my mother. So I don't. She continues to believe that her specific move was precisely predestined and foretold.

According to the skeptic's dictionary, cold reading refers to techniques used by professional manipulators (palm readers, psychics, fortune tellers, horoscope readers) to get a subject to think that the cold reader has some sort of special ability that allows him to 'mysteriously' know things about him or her. To the skeptic, the cold reader knows that his subject (the person being read) will be inclined to try to make sense out of whatever he or she is told no matter how vague or general.

This is a key point. We can't stop trying to make sense of events. That is the way our brains work. Our ancestors made sense of the weather by referring to the emotions of Gods. We try to make sense of our past, present and future, as well as other people's behavior. The cold reader takes advantage of this tendency. He knows that if he makes statements that appear meaningful, the subject will apply them to himself in a way that looks particularly insightful or revealing.

This is easy if the statement is vague enough and also inevitably true. Examples are: you will cross a body of water, sometimes you lack confidence, you will meet someone new, it takes effort to turn your dreams into reality, you have problems in an important relationship, etc. For the last statement, it is easy for the subject to be amazed and think, "My God, how did he know about the fight my boyfriend and I had about his pals coming to the movies with us?" Of course, the cold reader didn't. It is the subject who makes the connection between the vague statement and her own life circumstances.

The cold reader also knows that even if he makes several inaccurate statements about the subject, he will eventually make one that the subject can approve of and apply to himself or herself. He knows that the subject will remember the statements that the subject feels are relevant and forget the ones that the subject feels do not apply to him or her, because we look for and remember things that make sense to us.

Elinore was of course familiar with all this information. We spent a few minutes talking about people's need to have someone predict their future, even though they know that it is an impossible task. Elinore just shook her head sadly as she talked about the popularity of 1-800-call-a-psychic lines and of people wasting their money.

At 8 pm Dr. Brown arrived. After sitting down he explained that the cold reader who worked on campus for the last few weeks is 'hot'. Dr. Brown repeated his concern that the cold reader had developed a following of people who just go on and on about how terrific he is and spend hours discussing and analyzing his statements. There is disagreement in the administration about whether to do anything about the man who goes by the name, Mr. Fareye.

Some in the University administration argue his antics are just fun, he causes no harm, and people do not take him seriously. Besides, they say, some good might come from this. If the cold reader is deliberately vague, they reason, the subject will make his or her interpretation of what the cold reader means. In this way, they suggest, a visit to a cold reader (or psychic, or palm reader) may be a catalyst to a subject looking within and taking needed action. Often the action could be something she knows must be taken, but being human, has been procrastinating about.

For example, a subject may realize that he or she is in a relationship that has some major unresolved issues. The subject feels that something needs to be done. However, all the options are painful. Discussing difficult issues; ending a relationship; renegotiating a relationship; no one looks forward to doing any of this. It is hard and often painful work. So the subject procrastinates. The subject visits the cold reader, takes whatever is said in the way that his or her intuition knows it need to be taken, and takes the necessary action. Where is the harm, they tend to ask?

Dr. Brown explained that in his opinion, far from being harmless entertainment, this cold reading process may be damaging.

Students going to Mr. Fareye are likely to have real unresolved and troubling issues. They are likely to be vulnerable and confused. They will end up paying for a service that is useless. The harms do not stop there. The most likely candidates for real life problems are: relationship issues, health concerns, and money worries. These are the things that trouble people. The students are entitled to a thoughtful, competent, and responsible examination of these problems.

Those at the University who seek to expose Mr. Fareye desire that people get proper assistance with problems. Just like going to an unqualified medical practitioner might delay much needed appropriate medical treatment, going to an unqualified individual for personal advice might have the same effect. There was also concern that Mr. Fareye's practice was unregulated. If one feels incompetently treated by a medical doctor, a psychologist, or another professional, there is a regulatory body that one can ask to investigate. Where does one go if one feels that Mr. Fareye has messed up?

Due to this disagreement among the administration, a decision had been made to gather more data. Dr. Brown had asked Mr. Fareye for his cooperation in videotaping several of his sessions for analysis. Fareye had refused, saying that the 'bad vibes' from closed minds would interfere with his work. Dr. Brown then tried to negotiate for audio-taping but this idea was also rejected. Dr. Brown concluded by saying that the most Mr. Fareye would agree to was to have a neutral observer present for only one session.

Elinore and I had listened to this without any interruption. We looked at each other and I understood I was to be the observer.

Elinore said, "If you are up to it Mariah, we will take this on". I nodded agreement automatically. Right away the doubts crept in. I wondered how much could really be observed in just one session? Could I really observe anything useful?

Dr. Brown shuffled papers in his briefcase, and then stood up. "We need to move fast on this. We have a volunteer for the observation session. A social science student is most keen to see Mr. Fareye and has agreed to be accompanied on her session. My secretary will make the arrangements", he said as he went toward the door.

I met Joanna, the student, the next day in Mr. Fareye's waiting room. Joanna was an attractive blond with shoulder length straight hair, parted in the middle. She looked drawn and anxious. She was a bit pale. At about 5' 10" she loomed over me. Another look confirmed the initial sense of tension in her face and smile. She kept nervously tucking her hair behind her ears. I was a bit intimidated by this tall, fit beauty and wished I had worn a nicer outfit. We let out weak smiles. She spoke very little in the few minutes that we waited saying only that she really looked forward to this session and had some serious questions for which she needed answers.

I noticed she kept biting her nails, which were already bitten to the quick. She seemed to twitch and startle at every little noise.

Mr. Fareye turned out to be a well-groomed man of about 50. He had neatly trimmed gray hair and a full beard trimmed quite short. His accent was faintly British as he said, "good morning". He stood very straight and with exaggerated hand motions directed us to his inner sanctum. It was a small room with no windows. There was a central table with a dark tablecloth. There was a crystal vase with beautiful purple irises on the table. Soft classical music was playing.

He asked us to call him Max as he led me to a chair in the corner and then sat Joanna across from himself at the table. I felt embarrassed to be in on what seemed private. I tried to be silent and immobile, but I felt like a voyeur.

Max started off slowly and deliberately. He somehow managed to set an atmosphere of confident authority. I think it came from his formal posture and precise English diction. I scrawled my observations and comments as quickly as I could without taking my eyes off them. Max asked some general questions about Joanna's education, parents' work and religion.

To my surprise, Max was modest about his talents. He said that he was merely a channel receiving information from a higher source about Joanna's true character and future. He emphasized that he sometimes does not fully understand the communications that he receives. So it is really up to Joanna to strive to interpret the reading to her own life.

Joanna nodded to all this and just seemed eager to get on with it. Max then asked her permission to hold her right hand to help him receive her energies. She held out her hand and he lightly held her palm in his.

He then began the reading. "I feel that you have been thinking about a financial matter", he said. She did not respond verbally but I saw a tiny shake of the head indicating a no. I did not think Joanna knew that she had signaled a no. She seemed very passive waiting for him to lead.

Max quickly changed the topic. "I am getting a sense of you in an ambivalent relationship with a man". There was no reaction from Joanna. I am not getting a clear communication about the relationship, help me please", prompted Max.

Joanna seemed reluctant to answer but then in a weak and weary voice said, "yes, yes, there was a man who I had very strong feelings for but now the feelings are gone". She paused and then said in a barely audible voice, "but that is not my main reason for being here".

Smoothly Max responded, "I see that this is a painful area for you…something that you are not ready to deal with at this time…we truly should explore this further…(no verbal response from Joanna)…but I sense you are blocking…so we can't go there right now."

There was a long pause. Max seemed to be waiting for her to say why she had come if it wasn't about her relationship with the man. Finally, Joanna muttered, "it happened…my body did it…I was not sure…did not know what to do…". She was not making sense. She said nothing more. I was uncomfortable, wondering if I was interfering. I had to concentrate on observing and not give in to my desire to just close my eyes and thus give them more privacy. Max was studying Joanna's face. I was so glad that I was disciplined enough to keep on looking because of what happened next.

Max slowly said, "I am getting a feeling about a health concern". Joanna leaned forward and her left hand jumped to her abdomen. I do not think Joanna was aware of her hand movement but it was clear that Max did not miss it. He had certainly hit on something meaningful to Joanna. Perhaps not that surprising because of the strain I had noticed on her. Some major worry related to health was a probability. I was beginning to see the tricks of the cold readers trade.

"Yes, the health message is getting stronger. I think it involves you." A slight nod from Joanna. She certainly was not helping him much on an obvious level, but she was giving Max cues that he couldn't miss. Now I saw tears forming in her eyes. She was not sobbing, just wetness and redness was happening in her eyes. Max was still holding her right hand and watching her. Slowly he said, "Is your physical body gravely ill?" A slight shake of the head for no. I felt relieved. Joanna's left hand was still holding her abdomen. I was wondering…was she pregnant…was she considering an abortion? Max continued, "I find that nowadays not all young women aspire to be wives and mothers". Aha, Max and I were thinking along the same lines.

Joanna leaned back. I was learning now. Her movement away meant that a particular line did not grab her. Considering an abortion did not seem to be the thing on her mind. Max now leaned forward and I felt we were coming to the finale of the reading.

He continued holding her hand with his right and placed his left hand over the back of her right hand. Her right was sandwiched between his two. He dropped his voice deeper. "I get the feeling there is more, much more that you are not ready to deal with right now. That is fine. The thing is deep. I have a feeling it is more than your health... when you are ready...when you feel strong enough...you will be able to deal with it. I sense doubt and confusion in your soul." Then Max's voice went even deeper and slower so as to emphasize the next bit. *"I want you to keep in your thoughts the knowledge, the certain knowledge, that the mind has great power; greater power than we will ever know; the mind and body are connected; the mind has power over the body; you can use the power of your mind to accomplish what you need."*

At this Joanna started to cry with great heaving sobs. Max stopped talking but continued to hold Joanna's hand with one hand. He seemed very satisfied. Joanna cried for several minutes, a despairing cry, then she was spent. She pulled her hand away, put her shoulders back, wiped her face, stuck out her hand and shook his and thanked him profusely. She said she had got the exact answer to the question that had been troubling her. Some resolution had been arrived at in her mind. She left without a word or look at me.

I returned to describe the event and debrief with Elinore. I felt that there was not much that I could say. Yet Elinore praised me. "You did extremely well, you are a keen and objective witness," she said reassuringly. "Your observations are very helpful."

Nevertheless I could see Elinore was agitated. "What on earth did Joanna think Mr. Fareye told her?" she asked. "As far as I can tell he was wrong more often than right. He got off on the wrong track about finances and a relationship before he got to something about health. His style is not to ask a direct question yet he is effective in producing a response. For example, this line that 'I get a feeling about fill-in-the-blank' is very sneaky. If he is right, the subject gives him credit for special powers; if he is way off the mark he just slides to the next topic."

"He never commits himself. He gets feedback from her head nods/shakes, leaning in or away, voice tone, facial expression, posture, and so on. If he pays attention, he has a great opportunity to learn what the subject is or is not concerned about. Often a subject does not realize that she has 'answered' these promptings. After a suitable delay, Mr. Fareye could repeat what has been said or learned to the amazement of the subject."

"Wait a day for Joanna to reflect on the experience", continued Elinore, "call her tomorrow and see if she is willing to share with us."

It was not to be that way. The local hospital called late that night with the shocking news that Joanna had taken a drug overdose in an apparent suicide attempt. She was still at the hospital, out of danger after having her stomach pumped. She was asking to see me. Elinore and I jumped into her car.

Joanna was lying in a bed in a private room. There was an intravenous line in her arm and she was hooked up to a heart monitor. The monitor was beeping away disclosing her heart rate. Joanna looked somehow thinner and even paler than at the reading. She was crying.

"I am so glad you are getting care", I said, "but what caused you to do this?"

"I knew I killed her, I always knew it", she cried, "Max confirmed it for me." The sobbing increased as did the rate of the beeping. "I killed my baby", she was wracked by sobs, "I knew it from the moment it happened. I tried to deny it to myself but with Max's help I know I can't hide from knowing it".

Alarmingly, the beeping was becoming extremely rapid. I snuck a look at the monitor's display. Her heart rate was 162 per minute. This was surely not good.

Just then, a nurse rushed into the room. She glanced at us and said, "I am afraid you are upsetting the patient!"

Elinore drew out her wallet and showed her psychologist identification. Speaking both to the nurse and to Joanna she said in an authoritative yet calm voice, "I am taking responsibility for Joanna. Please leave us so that we can work through her troubles and put this load of fear and guilt behind her. She has been very brave and decisive. Now she needs to think."

With this she approached, looked at her kindly and said, "I know you have been through something difficult. I think there are issues it may be helpful to discuss. Right now. Let's talk it through. Do you want to work on this now?" Joanna nodded.

Elinore looked at the nurse and I, almost willing us to leave. The nurse looked doubtful. I looked at the heart rate monitor read-out. During Elinore's speech the reading had dropped from 162 to 128. The nurse followed my eyes. She sighed and left. I followed her out, closing the door behind me and went to the waiting area.

Elinore came out of the room two hours later. She asked me to say goodnight to Joanna. I was stunned. Joanna was looking less frantic and maybe even a tiny bit relieved. The heart rate monitor was rock steady at 89 beats per minute. Not terrific but vastly improved from earlier in the night. I wished Joanna a peaceful night and went home with Elinore.

Elinore did not wait for my questions. "This was a most instructive experience", she said. "I have never before counseled a person who was hooked up to a heart monitor. Whenever I said something that was sensitive or painful to her, I could see and hear the rate go up. If I said something that she felt was reassuring the rater dropped. The equipment should be standard in all psychologist's offices", she joked. "If clients are deceptive or just out of touch with their true feelings, this equipment would give the psychologist a chance."

"Joanna told me her story. She has no relatives in the vicinity. She came here three years ago to study and work. She met a man and has been in an exclusive relationship with him for three years. The relationship has some good points and some serious difficulties. The man abuses alcohol and drugs and although he treats her well when he is not under the influence, she knows he is neither stable nor reliable enough to be counted on for being a life partner nor a father. She had just decided to leave him when she discovered she was pregnant."

"The pregnancy changed everything for her. She does not believe in abortion. She felt that she had to make the relationship work. She knew she would care for the baby but the thought of being in a relationship with the father for life seemed distinctly undesirable. She did not want to become a single mother. She did not want to find another man, just so her child could have a father. She was stuck. She spent several nights thinking about how nice it would be to not be pregnant. A few days later she started to bleed and experienced a miscarriage."

"She believed she had killed her baby by not wanting it and this thought was confirmed by whatever happened with Max, you know that bit about the mind is powerful and the mind and the body are connected. The guilt was overwhelming. As a murderer, she saw no way out but to kill herself."

"How did you help her?", I asked

"First I calmed her down. Then I used your observations. I explained to her that Max, whether he realizes it or not, is a fake. He hit the three main themes that people are troubled by: finances, relationships, and health. He got his two initial tries wrong, but of course she forgot about that. Joanna saw her issue as one of health. In her mind, her negative thoughts about the pregnancy had caused her body to react 'unhealthily' and expel the fetus. I described to her how her mostly nonverbal feedback to Max could be read by nearly anyone. It surely did not take special powers to understand a nod or shake of the head, tension in her hand, and sobbing. Joanna gave Max a useful clue when her left hand moved to her lower abdomen as he was talking about health. Max had done no better than any careful observer."

"The most impact on Joanna though came as we went over Max's final words. The ones about the mind and the body being connected and the power of the mind over the body. Joanna interpreted this as confirmation that she had killed the fetus. I gently pointed out to her that it was her mind that had made the connection between his words and her miscarriage. Mr. Fareye had never uttered the words: pregnancy, unwanted child, abortion, miscarriage, or murder!"

"Had Joanna suffered an illness from which she was well on the road to recovery, she could easily interpret his words as indicating that she was doing well on the mental front and healing herself. Had she been ill and getting worse, she could interpret his words as indicating that she was not disciplined enough about controlling her negative thoughts."

"The thing is that the statement the mind and the body are connected is of course true and important to bear in mind. We saw that, when she was hooked up to the heart monitor. Emotion was reflected in her heart rate. Yet what does this statement mean about her miscarriage? Does it really mean that a woman who truly does not want to give birth will miscarry? Of course not, there are many counterexamples! Does it mean that a woman who truly wants the child will not miscarry? Of course, not! However, the utterly sleazy thing about the statement is that it can never be proven wrong! It is so vague that whatever happens can be taken as confirmation of its truth and of Mr. Fareye's powers".

I could see that Elinore was seething with anger. She went to her liquor cabinet and poured herself something big. She downed it quickly and then said in a slightly despairing tone, "Oh Mariah, I think that some bad ideas will never die. The belief in psychic powers is just one example."

"Anyway, giving birth and raising a child is a big project. Anyone is bound to have both positive and negative feelings about it. So any woman who miscarries can think about some speck of doubt she had. And any woman who carries the child to full-term can feel that her positive thoughts outweighed the negative. The statement the mind and the body are connected, as applied to miscarriage can never possibly be proven to be wrong for a specific woman, no matter what the relationship between mind and body. In scientific language, it is not a falsifiable claim. Fortunately, Joanna had enough psychology and science courses that once she thought about it she immediately recognized that the statement was meaningless in application to her miscarriage."

"I also explained to Joanna that many miscarriages are nature's way of handling pregnancies in which there is some physical abnormality with the fetus. Her partner's substance abuse may well have affected his sperm, causing a developmental problem. She had not thought of that angle. By the way, Joanna has asked to come and see me for several more sessions."

"We have earned our sleep for tonight. Tomorrow we see Mr. Fareye". Next morning I called to make the arrangements. The answering machine declared, "Mr. Max Foreye, the renowned reader, had been invited by his many appreciative clients to undertake an international tour of lectures and readings". We never saw him again.

----

1. What are some of the intended messages of this fable?
2. What errors in critical thinking did Joanna make?
3. Describe how Joanna's selective attention to the words of Mr. Fareye contributed to hindsight bias and confirmation bias.
4. What typical human thinking errors does Max Fareye take advantage of (intentionally or not)?
5. Can you think of situations where similar failures in critical thinking can lead to bad outcomes? Does this fable resonate with any story or experience that you may have been involved with or heard about?
6. In the fable Mr. Fareye is presented as not having any psychic powers. Do you agree or disagree with that perception? You can disagree with the intended message, but if you take that track you need to, like all students, present a reasoned and coherent argument to support your views.
7. Many students feel that some psychics are 'fakes' but that a few could have powers that are as yet unverifiable. If you think this way consider: of what use is an unverifiable power?

2.

Almost Abducted by Aliens

We had spent two quiet weeks without a new case. Elinore reported that Joanna's mood was improving but Elinore was concerned that she could easily relapse. While waiting for the next case, Elinore had suggested some interesting books. I particularly enjoyed *Believing in Magic: the Psychology of Superstition*. This book explains how otherwise smart and rational people can put their faith in silly superstitions. I could tell Elinore was getting restless and was impatient for a new case. There was little of the positive excitement that I had seen on her while she was working.

Therefore it was with some anticipation that I now observed Elinore on the phone. The emotional flatness of her face was being replaced by animation. Her head nods, shakes and smiles were becoming energized. It was a curious thing, I thought, that she put so much energy into facial expressions and gestures that the person on the other end of the line could not possibly see.

Once off the phone, she turned to me and speaking rapidly told me that we had a new referral. Dr. Susan Hanson, a professor has asked to see us. Dr. Hanson's 12 year old son, Tom, developed sudden severe anxiety and social withdrawal after seeing something unusual in the sky. Dr. Hanson was on her way.

"I believe that you are not interested in ordinary clinical work. Am I incorrect?" I asked Elinore, surprised that she would take on such a routine matter.

"You are right in the sense that I have little interest in trying to readjust the emotions of this boy. Here it appears that we have a normal boy who had a sudden emotional change as a result of seeing something. I am not busy and I think there may be features of interest in this case", she replied. "I am truly curious about what this boy saw and what he is thinking about it, and I am especially curious how his thoughts play on his emotions."

Half an hour later our visitor arrived. She was a woman in her mid 40s, fair-haired and rather pale. She was wringing her hands, blinking rapidly, and her breathing was shallow. After the brief introductions, Elinore asked her to describe what had brought her to us.

It took her a visible effort to take a deep breath, sit straight, and put her shoulders back. She began. "Tom is my only child. He is 12 and has always been a quiet, reasonable and cooperative boy. He has fine friends and has always been a good student. He has never been in trouble and he always seemed sensible. He just doesn't flip out, even when his friends do. I have always trusted him completely. Last Saturday, he was on his way home from a friend's house. It was about 9 pm and just getting dark. He was riding his bicycle, even though he was not supposed to at night, and he was taking a shortcut along the bluffs overlooking the ocean.

"It was there that he describes seeing five spheres flying in formation above him. There was a blue metallic glow emanating from each of the spheres. That unnatural glow really convinced him these were alien craft. The five spheres were identical. There were neither windows on them nor any discernible external features such as wings or engines. Nor was there any engine sound or any other sound of movement through the air. There was also no sonic boom, which Tom specifically expected due to the spheres' high rate of speed. Tom also remarked on the ability of the spheres to change speed and direction suddenly, far more sharply than possible for any human-made craft. It was difficult to tell size, but Tom thinks the spheres were the size of a passenger jet."

Dr. Hanson paused, took another deep breath and then continued. "Tom said his reaction was absolute fright. He was alone on the bluff, it was dark, and the spheres were maneuvering over him. He said he observed for about a minute, then wheeled his bike under the lone large tree on that section of the bluff. He felt that the aliens would be less likely to detect him under the tree. However, in a few seconds he realized that the spheres were heading lower and toward him. He then understood that the tree was going to provide scant protection from advanced space aliens able to create these spheres."

"So he hopped on his bike and raced home at top speed. He was sure the space beings were going to attempt to abduct him."

Dr. Hanson explained that Tom had sometimes watched TV programs about aliens, flying saucers, and psychic phenomena. She tried to reduce his exposure to these irresponsible media representations and to debrief with him if he did watch but it was not always possible. Anyway, Tom had made fun of these kinds of programs and their nonsense. However, on that bluff, Tom came to believe, and still does believe that aliens saw him, were targeting him for abduction, and will try again.

Tom has refused to leave the house in the five days since. He also refuses to talk on the phone as he believes that the aliens will be able to trace his calls and nab him. He is alone in his room reading magazines about aliens. Of course, he has not been to school. Two of his friends came over once but they left after a short time. No one else has come. Tom is completely isolated, he does not eat or sleep properly, and he is convinced that if he makes one mistake the aliens will be able to locate and abduct him.

As a first step in getting help, Dr. Hanson had called a counselor. The counselor had been specific. His advice was for the family to support Tom, accept his version of the events, and acknowledge to Tom the fearfulness of the events. The counselor felt that Tom should not be forced to go for counseling. He felt that unquestioning emotional support for what Tom was going through was the key thing to helping him. "You must repeatedly acknowledge how frightening this experience must be for him", he had advised. When Dr. Hanson mentioned her worries about Tom's social isolation he said, "you must accept his need for privacy at this scary time". He repeated the need to "accept where Tom is at now" in terms of his emotions and how he spends his time. The counselor said there was a need to "affirm and validate" Tom's experience and not doubt it, as any questioning would further weaken his sense of self and of trust in adults.

Dr. Hanson indicated she is reluctant to follow this advice because she cannot see how leaving him alone with his thoughts will help resolve the situation. She also could not stand to see Tom suffer this way. With this she slumped and looked toward Elinore and then me with hopeful and pleading eyes.

I also looked at Elinore to see how she would approach this situation. Her face was alert. It was clear that she was going to rise to the challenge. "Dr. Hanson", she began, "you are to be commended for taking concrete steps to help your son. There is in fact something crucial that needs to be explained about his observations. I am sure that Tom reported accurately the stimuli that reached his retina. Whether he perceived those stimuli accurately is what we must study."

"I also must frankly tell you that I disagree with the advice of the counselor. In my view, Tom is not frightened by the sensations that reached his retina from the stimulus in the sky. He is frightened by the perceptions, the interpretations, his brain made of those stimuli. This is a subtle but crucial distinction. Imagine that you are walking in the woods in bear territory. You hear a rustle behind some bushes. It could be a small bird, or it could be a bear. It is not the rustle that scares, any scaring is done by what you think it is. That is by your interpretations of the rustle. So, I would prefer to work on what Tom's thoughts are, and on the basis for those thoughts. I would prefer this approach rather than reinforcing his feelings, which might be based on erroneous perceptions and thoughts." I did not think Elinore's approach could be put any more starkly. Dr. Hanson nodded. She straightened a bit. I could see this made sense to her.

Elinore turned to me and swung into action. "Mariah, there are some things I need you to do. Go over to Dr. Hanson's house. See Tom. In other circumstances, I would have said to phone, but obviously he would think that is risky. Let Tom know that a serious investigation is under way. Treat him respectfully of course. Let him know that his report is being taken seriously, yet his perceptions need further study. Ask him to draw you a map of the bluff, marking the place he was when he first saw the spheres, the tree that he briefly sheltered under and the other major features of the location."

"After that, I want you to get some more information. First from the weather office find out the wind direction, speed, whether the skies were clear or overcast, and range of visibility last Saturday at 9pm; second, I want you to go to the particular tree tomorrow during the day and report back to me about anything special about the tree or under the tree; and third, I want you to go back near the tree at about 9pm and look to see if there are any bright sources of light, especially blue light, in the area."

I was excited. Elinore was fully engaged with this matter. I was being needed again. Parts of the episode with Joanna had been uncomfortable for me. My role here seemed easier. On the ride with Dr. Hanson, I could sense her anxiety. She was a conscientious mother. She wanted to do the right thing. Nothing in her life had prepared her to deal with this.

Tom turned out to be a short boy with many freckles. As soon as he understood that I was approaching the event with a serious and open mind he was keen to talk. He presented the observations logically and precisely. He was pleased to have me ask relevant questions that implied he was being taken seriously and not being considered crazy or foolish. He gladly drew the map. At the end of our talk, he asked me if I believed him about Saturday night. The question put me on the spot. I wanted to let him know that he was a trusted witness, while at the same time letting him know that the meaning we draw from events is always subjective and open to various interpretations.

After some hesitation, I looked him straight in the eye. Neither of us blinked as I said, "I trust that what you have said is an honest description of what you saw. My job is to understand what was going on." I felt this answer skillfully validated his experience while introducing the idea that what he believed he had seen was not the only explanation. He seemed satisfied with my response. He asked me several thoughtful questions about what else he could have seen. I could not answer but I left feeling comfortable that this meeting had gone well.

The weather office reported that the wind was from the west (off the ocean onto shore) at about 15 miles an hour. They also said that there had been very light, diffuse low cloud cover on Saturday night resulting in limited visibility of about 1 mile, at 9 pm.

I reported this to Elinore the next morning and showed her Tom's drawing. There was no reaction other than a small nod and the hint of a smile. Later in the afternoon, just as I was about to head out the door to inspect the tree the phone rang. It was Dr. Hanson. Tom was still frightened of using the phone himself but he did have a request. Could he accompany me to inspect the tree? Dr. Hanson was happy. Not only had Tom talked to me the evening before, putting at least a pause in his social isolation, he had slept better and seemed more at ease. Also, this would be the first time Tom would leave the house in six days. Dr. Hanson was encouraged as was I.

Dr. Hanson drove but stayed in the car. The tree was a solitary tree, about 60 feet high, about 30 feet back from the edge of the bluff. We searched around the base and under the tree. No sign of any craft landing there. No circular depressions, no scorched earth. Just many bird feathers and bird droppings. Tom and I studied all these signs and after 20 minutes we returned to the car. Back home, I reported all this to Elinore. She seemed contented. In the evening I did my only remaining task. I walked the neighborhood near the bluff. Aside from a few street and house lights, the only major light source was a huge neon advertising sign on the lot of the local car dealer. It was multicolored, with a deep blue dominating.

Two nights later Elinore, Dr. Hanson, Tom, and I were sitting under the tree at 8:45 pm. Tom was munching on the remains of a pizza. Elinore had asked that we gather here on the first overcast night with low diffuse cloud cover and wind off the ocean. Tom's curiosity had overcome his fear. As the darkness deepened I saw the excitement of anticipation on Elinore's face. And then, just before 9 pm, it happened. This time only four metallic spheres appeared in formation. They were glowing a deep metallic blue. We watched them maneuver exactly as Tom had described. We watched for about a minute with my heart pounding with increasing fear. Just as I was ready to run for it in an amazing moment, all four spheres simultaneously flapped their wings. They were birds.

Later, amid relief and laughter back at our house we debriefed. Elinore said, "These birds soared in formation on the wind blown up over the bluff. There was no need for wing flapping. Due to the overcast, the moon and the stars could not be seen. So we had no cues for distance, for how far away the objects were. Tom and the rest of us assumed that the objects were much farther than they actually were. They were actually barely above tree top height. But since we perceived them as being several miles up, we assumed they were the size of a plane. A bird at treetop height takes up the same arc on our retina as a jetliner at 30,000 feet. Because we assumed they were miles away, we attributed far more speed to them than their actual speed. Their apparent abrupt changes of direction seemed impossible for earthly objects of that great size and speed."

We realized that at dusk, they came in off the sea. The bluffs were an ideal place for soaring. They soared on the wind for a few minutes before coming in to roost on the tree. Tom laughed. "I got it. Being sea birds, the underneath parts were still wet. The blue neon advertising sign reflected off their wet parts, making them look shiny, glowing and metallic. Also, when they came toward the tree I had hidden under, it had nothing to do with me. It is a great place to roost for the night. The birds and I were both looking for shelter and found it at about the same time. Because I was so frightened the first time, I had not stayed long enough to see them flapping their wings as they came in to roost on the tree. Oh man, I am so glad we figured it out."

Later that evening, Elinore and I were picking at pieces of cheese and drinking a glass of white wine. Actually I was drinking a glass, she was on her third one. Elinore was in an ebullient mood. "I am so glad you we did this one together Mariah. This case has illustrative features. We found out the reason that Tom perceived what he did. Can you imagine the outcome, if Tom had been approached on an emotional level only? If people had said they loved him, understood him, accepted him, and had empathy for the fears that he has? And just stopped there?"

"He needed to know what was going on. Since we found out they were birds, nothing has changed in the sensations reaching his retina. If he went back there tomorrow night, he might see exactly what he saw the first night. What has changed are his thoughts. He knows they are birds not aliens out to abduct him. This knowledge changes his emotions from fear to delight. Too often, we try to deal with feelings without acknowledging that these feelings are rooted in thoughts. I keep repeating this idea but hardly anyone listens to me. To understand emotions, people need to examine their thoughts, not just their emotions alone.

"At another level", Elinore continued, "there are more significant features. If we encounter an odd phenomenon in psychology, we need to look at all the commonplace, known, usual mechanisms that may bring the phenomenon about, before we look for bizarre explanations. Too many people are willing to believe in space aliens, psychic phenomena, horoscopes, and so on without looking for ordinary and logical explanations."

"Take this case. As soon as I heard that silent objects moving in formation in the sky needed to be explained, I thought of what most commonly would meet these criteria? Birds! So how to understand no flapping of wings? Soaring! I sent you to get wind information. Misperceptions of size, distance and speed? Might be a lack of cues about distance that most commonly occur in diffused cloudy conditions."

"The metallic blue shine? What else but a reflection from below? I sent you to locate the source. When you found feathers and bird droppings under the tree, I was nearly certain. The only other likely suspects would have been kites. They fly, they are silent, they change direction rapidly. But the boy saw no one else there and it is difficult to fly that many kites in formation. No, each of the boy's observations were individually suggestive of birds, together with your information they had a cumulative force pointing to birds alone."

I went to bed thinking about the linkages between thoughts and emotions in my own life.

----

1. Discuss the role of top-down processing in Tom's initial interpretation that these were alien craft. How might 'perceptual set' be involved here?

2. In terms of bottom-up processing how available were usual cues to size, distance and speed in Tom's initial observations? Which normal cues were missing? How might the limitations of available cues for distance contribute to his initial perception that these were aliens?

3. It is not too soon to start thinking about the relationship between thought and emotion. How are they related? Does one of them come first? Which one? Can you think of an example of a thought leading to a strong emotion and you later finding the thought was in error?

4. Have you had experiences in which about perceptual illusions played a role?

3.

MOODY (FE)MALES ?

Elinore and I basked in the satisfaction of the clean way we had handled Tom's perceptions. We were getting to be known as a team. Therefore I was not surprised when Elinore mentioned we had received another referral. I was confused that she had accepted what looked like another clinical case, this time a marital difficulty involving our Dr. Brown and his wife.

Elinore had obtained his permission for me to sit in on the sessions. She had winked at me in a mischievous way. "This promises to be revealing." I knew there were some differences in attitude and some competitiveness between her and Dr. Brown. I also knew that they needed each other. She needed the referrals and he knew she was the best. Elinore filled in some details about Dr. Brown. He was trained as a biologist. He had then moved into university administration.

I could not imagine having any credibility on marriage issues with people who had been in a relationship for as long as I had been alive. I asked to be a silent observer. I could not imagine Elinore being a head-nodding, affirming, ever-patient, always supportive, therapist. I wanted to see how she approached the situation.

After he sat down, Elinore asked him how we could help. "I have come to you for advice. It is about my wife and our relationship. We have been married for 20 years. It has always troubled me that she has such severe premenstrual symptoms (PMS). For at least a week, sometimes 10 days before her periods she is irritable, has huge mood swings, picks fights with me. At these times she is just miserable and miserable to be with. I feel completely helpless at these times. Nothing I do seems to help. I think she is in denial about this problem."

Good, I thought to myself, he seems open. Also bad, he thinks of his wife as a biological organism. He has not mentioned anything of her thoughts, her possible feelings, or his role in the marriage relationship.

Elinore took a slow breath, "You have lived with this for 20 years, what brings this to a head now?"

"We both suffer and our relationship is going downhill. It is past time to deal with this. I am tired of trying to work it out on my own."

"Oh dear, oh dear", Elinore sympathized with some veiled irony. "You poor man, you are truly a prince of patience. But do tell, how have you coped with these horrible hormonal hurricanes all these years?" He was expecting support, so he responded to the supportive tone, totally missing the hidden sarcasm of the words.

"I have worked hard, and been at the lab a great deal of the time. I also arrange to do activities with my friends, away from home when my wife is going through these difficult times," he replied.

"I see, so you remove yourself when the situation gets difficult", noted Elinore.

"As much as possible, but of course I really did have to work very long hours to succeed at my career."

Elinore leaned forward, "So, just to make sure I have it right, you believe that your wife's moods are influenced by her hormonal levels. These cause her to be miserable and upset at certain times and make your relationship with her rocky."

"Exactly," he looked relieved to be so well understood.

"I do need clarification about a couple of things," Elinore continued. "How do you know when your wife is premenstrual? Do you specifically ask her?"

Dr. Brown looked puzzled. "No, I don't need to ask. I can tell by her moods and behavior."

"That is what I needed to clarify," responded Elinore. "So you see her upset and you assume it is that time of the month. Based on your interpretation of past experience, you decide it is not a great time to be together. You leave. Possibly you let her know in some additional nonverbal way that she is not fit company for you at present. You return home a few hours later, still avoiding her because you are convinced she is in a bad mood."

"What surprises me about all this is the circularity of it all", she continued. "How do you know she is premenstrual? Because she is in a bad mood! Why is she in a bad mood? Because she is premenstrual! Would it not have been better to gather each set of data independently? That is to chart her cycles and her moods. That way you could compare the menstrual and mood data and determine if there is a relationship. It would even be better if she charted her cycle and you charted her moods without knowing the stage of her cycle. There would be less opportunity for your expectation to influence your perceptions and ratings. Wouldn't you ask your students to work this way if they were trying to understand associations between two variables?"

"Certainly I would do that if we were working on new research," agreed Dr. Brown. "However in this instance it is not necessary to do the controlled data collection that you suggest. Everyone knows of the relationship between hormone levels and mood," he said a trifle testily.

"And everyone knows that 'absence makes the heart go fonder' just as much as they know that 'out of sight is out of mind'. And everyone is sure that 'opposites attract' while 'birds of a feather flock together'. I am afraid, Dr. Brown that often what everyone thinks they know is of little value in understanding some kinds of human behavior. We are set up to look for evidence that confirms what we already believe rather than noticing evidence that disconfirms our existing beliefs."

"For example," Elinore continued, "let us examine some of the beliefs that you have about your wife's hormones and moods. You believe that you have noticed a relationship but we know that your evidence for a relationship is very weak. You have neglected to look for evidence that may not support your hypothesis. Specifically, you have not thought about the possibility that most people, female or male, have mood changes. Are you sure that hers are larger or more frequent than yours?"

"Have you thought about the possibility that her changes in mood may have other causes separate from hormonal influences? Reflecting on what you have described I can immediately think of a hypothesis. You think she is premenstrual, so you avoid her and subtly signal your disapproval of her. Would not your mood be affected if someone you loved treated you that way?"

Dr. Brown scratched his head. He gave me an odd look. He shifted uneasily in his chair, but did not say anything.

"Look, we need more data," she said in her direct way. "I am going to ask you to keep a record of your wife's moods on a questionnaire called the *Menstrual Distress Questionnaire* (MDQ). This is a widely used method of evaluating the effects of menstrual symptoms on women." She went to her desk and pulled out a huge pile of forms. "As you can see," she continued as she showed him one of the questionnaires, "the subjects are asked to rate symptoms on a 6-point scale ranging from 'no experience of the symptom' to 'disabling experience of the symptom'."

As Dr. Brown studied one of the forms, I took one. Nearly all of the possible symptoms were negative: moodiness, discomfort, depression, cramps, back pains, food craving, irritability, water retention, headaches, and so on. There was no way to record any positive moods. I wondered about the implicit biases of those who had designed the questionnaire.

Elinore waited until Dr. Brown looked up. "I have decided what data we need. I would like you to ask your wife to fill out one of these forms each day, noting on the form the stage of her menstrual cycle as well. On identical forms, I am going to ask you to rate your wife every day. Now, obviously there are some questions, like the ones about cramps and water retention, that you can't rate her on. Leave those private symptoms that are not accessible to you out. Just do the ones that you can. I want you to do this for two complete months. There will be 60 sets of ratings by your wife and 60 by you, one each for the 60 days.

It is crucial to follow proper procedure. So, I am asking you to fill out the ratings for your wife without asking her about the timing of her cycle. It must be done that way to minimize the effects of expectations on your ratings." She handed him the pile of forms.

"And the rest of the forms?" inquired Dr. Brown looking at another pile of the same height as the one he just received.

"Those are about you," smiled Elinore. "Yes, I want you to fill out the *Menstrual Distress Questionnaire* with respect to yourself. Obviously you do not have periods. Possibly, you may experience mood changes and physical symptoms over the two months. It would be informative to collect the relevant data. I am going to ask you to rate yourself and to independently have your wife rate you. Some questions won't apply to you but many will. The ones about moods and headaches and backaches are ones you could be rated on. I think it would be valuable to have some idea of the variability of your moods and physical changes as compared to your wife's. So far you have assumed that she is the only one of you two who changes with time or experiences negative symptoms and moods.

"You want me to do this for two months?" he asked.

"Yes please. I am sympathetic to your ongoing marital problems, but I need data before I can be of further help."

We set an appointment time two months ahead and Dr. Brown took his leave.

We did not hear from Dr. Brown over the next two months. Elinore and I did not discuss the issues until the day of the scheduled appointment. She set up a time for she and I to meet two hours prior to the appointment with Dr. Brown. She had the completed questionnaires in four piles. "I have asked a student studying statistics to go through these responses", she explained.

"We have four sets of ratings; Mrs. Brown's self-ratings, Dr. Brown's ratings of Mrs. Brown; Dr. Brown's self-ratings and Mrs. Brown's ratings of him. I have asked a statistician to summarize the data. She has calculated a daily 'physical distress score' by adding together all the physical symptom scores for that day (headaches, backache, etc). I have asked for one other daily score; an 'emotional distress score' obtained by adding together the ratings for irritability, negative moods, and so on."

"I am not so much interested in the actual scores as I am in the patterns. I am curious to see if Mrs. Brown's self-ratings do have a relationship with stage of her menstrual cycle. I am interested to see if his ratings of her correlate with her menstrual cycle. The thing that I have been most keen to see though is his self-ratings and Mrs. Brown's ratings of him. I wondered if he really would demonstrate more mood stability than she."

She was in her lecture mode. I sat and listened. "This is such an interesting field," she began. "It is known that people of both sexes experience hormonal variations and cycles. However, only women demonstrate clear physical signs of their hormonal cycles. That may be one of the reasons why nearly everything negative that women feel or do, has at one time or another, been attributed to hormonal changes. The lack of outward saliency of men's hormonal changes may be one reason why we do not attribute all negative male moods and behaviors to their hormones."

I interrupted "Elinore, what is the difference in hormone levels between men and women?"

"Sorry, I guess I need to back up" Elinore said helpfully. "Estrogens are a group of hormones that have effects on sexual development and cycles primarily in women; while androgens are a group of hormones that effect what are considered male sexual characteristics and development. Many people assume that estrogen is present only in females and androgens only in males. However, both hormones are present in both sexes although it is true that females have much higher levels of estrogens and males have higher levels of androgens. There are many hormones involved with maturation and reproduction in both women and men, so that talking about one 'female' and 'male' hormone is an oversimplification."

"A related problem is that without taking daily blood samples and measuring the levels of hormones, we just do not know how much of a particular hormone is present in a person's blood at a specific time. So in assuming hormone and mood relationships, we are looking for links between variables even though we are very uncertain about the variables themselves."

"Keep in mind, Mariah, that in many cultures menstruation is enmeshed in a context of negative and shameful associations. So, it may be that women feel negative premenstrually for mainly social rather than hormonal reasons. Indeed, when women are asked to rate their daily moods in relation to their periods, a pattern of association between negative moods and the premenstrual part of the cycle is observed."

"Amazingly, surprisingly, and to many people unbelievably, research that has asked women to rate their daily moods over time (with no mention of menstrual period, and no suggestion that the research involves menstruation) found no link between reports of mood and the menstrual cycle! This is an astounding finding!"

Elinore continued, "most people don't catch the significance of this finding the first time they hear of it. Some people refuse to believe these findings even though they are quite clear. Let me repeat it for you. If women rate their moods without knowing that the research involves menstrual cycles, practically no correlation is found between mood and stage of menstrual cycle for the vast majority of women. However, if the researchers are interested in menstrual cycles and mood, a link is found. This suggests that women's expectation plays a significant role in the perceived link. Of course, no one questions that women experience physical symptoms", she finished.

"In other kinds of studies, called 'retrospective studies' the subjects do not keep ongoing records. They are asked to recall how they felt at particular times. In these types of studies we find particularly strong associations between being premenstrual and being in low mood. What does that suggest to you, Mariah?" she asked me suddenly.

I was attempting to pull all this information together. "Possibly that when we recall things we are selective," I started tentatively. "We may remember particularly awful moods and if we have menstruation on our minds we are more likely to remember bad times that occurred premenstrually than other bad times, creating the illusion of a strong relationship where in fact only a small one might exist. We might not recall times when we felt good premenstrually." I thought I finished on some strong points.

"Exactly what I think!" she answered. "There is one more piece of research that I want you to consider before we look at the Brown's data. Rarely are men asked to keep a record of their mood swings and outbursts. But on the few occasions that such information has been collected, the swings men exhibit over time are at least equal in size to those displayed by women. I wonder why we never hear about that?"

After letting that question hang in the air, she showed me the statistical summary of Dr. and Mrs. Brown's data. It had been summarized in two figures. The first was for Mrs. Brown and had the 60 days along the horizontal axis. The days of her cycle were marked. Along the vertical axis was marked "distress rating". There were four irregular lines. These were marked: self-rated emotional distress, self-rated physical distress, emotional distress as rated by husband, and physical distress as rated by husband.

Her physical distress self-ratings were strongly related to stage of the menstrual cycle. That is, she felt physically way worse premenstrually than at other times. However, her emotional distress was only slightly related, way less than the physical ratings, to stage of menstrual cycle. His ratings of her, showed very little link. There was a tiny relationship between stage of her menstrual cycle and his rating of her physical distress; no relationship at all between his ratings of her emotional distress and stage of menstrual cycle.

The second figure was for Dr. Brown. It was set up the same way; the days along the horizontal axis and measure of distress along the vertical axis. He also had the four irregular lines. His self-ratings, although showing no monthly pattern, showed irregular and frequent variations in both emotional and physical distress. The variations were slightly larger than hers. Mrs. Brown's ratings of him were similar to his own ratings most of the time.

As I was thinking about this, there was a knock on the door. To our surprise, Dr. and Mrs. Brown had both come. After they sat down, Elinore went over the figures with them. She explained that the relationship between being premenstrual and distress displayed on Mrs. Brown's self-ratings may be partially attributable to expectation or to other non-hormonal factors.

Elinore explained her understanding of the research on this point. Elinore felt that the most carefully done studies on women's moods could find little or no evidence that irritability, poor self-esteem, and depression were more common premenstrually than at any other time. She emphasized that physical symptoms are certainly related; emotional symptoms weakly, if at all.

Supporting her interpretation are studies that find that women who retrospectively (that is looking back on events in their past) indicated that they were most likely to have emotional upsets just before their periods turned out not to have that pattern when they kept ongoing records of mood without any reference to menstrual cycle.

"Of course", Elinore added, "we have support for this idea of expectation being involved from the data. Dr. Brown rated Mrs. Brown without knowledge of her hormonal state and his data indicate no connection between her menstrual cycle and his ratings of her distress. However, Mrs. Brown, who knows when she was premenstrual and knew that was an area of our concern, could not avoid being influenced by expectation and perceived a slight relationship."

Both the Browns studied the figures without any comment. I wondered if they were overwhelmed by the data. Dr. Brown would be used to interpreting these figures but I wondered if Mrs. Brown could make sense of it all. I need not have worried. It was she who took the lead.

"Look, dear," she picked up both figures. She traced some of the sections of his and her ratings with her forefinger. "You actually have more and larger mood swings and about the same number of physical changes as I do."

He looked, "Right, I can see that," he said a little defensively. "There are explanations, though," he continued. "Day 12, was the day after I played way too much tennis. My knees, elbow, and back hurt. I guess I am not as fit as I thought. And day 19, was when I found out that a crucial experiment that we had invested a lot of time and effort into had to be abandoned because some thoughtless person contaminated the samples. No wonder I was irritable and upset. You must understand, anyone would be. The same goes for most of the other spikes in my physical or emotional distress. There is a rational explanation for each. Please understand that," he said.

She was sharper and tougher than I thought. "Yes, dear I can. But you know", she started innocently, "there is something that I do have trouble understanding. How is it that when you have mood swings or pains, there is an external event that causes it?"

"Because there is", he replied.

"Yet, if I have a mood swing it is automatically attributed to my internal states, to my hormones? Do you not think I have disappointments, difficult relationships, unexpected setbacks? Whenever you behave or feel badly you know an external cause. And whenever, I have a difficult time you appear to think or know the internal cause within me. How come? Do you not think, dear, that possibly you are being a tiny bit self-serving?"

To his credit, Dr. Brown did not dismiss her. He picked up the graphs and studied them carefully. "The data is revealing", he said to Elinore. I have a lot to think about and my wife and I have a lot to discuss. He turned to Mrs. Brown , "I am seeing things in a new light as a result of this data and discussion. I think there is a lot here for me to try to understand."

"That is an excellent idea", she said happily. "However, I will have to study your chart very carefully to see if you can be rational and communicative at this time. We certainly do not want to start out on such a sensitive task at a bad time of the month for you!"

----

1. What processes of attention and memory may lead to a perceived exaggeration of the any relationship between mood and menstrual cycle?

2. Describe more specifically how the above processes could lead to the illusion of a correlation between mood and menstrual cycle.

3. When we make a judgment about the cause of a mood or behavior, we are making an 'attribution'. An attribution explains why a particular behavior occurring. We may attribute causes of behavior to internal causes in the person doing the behavior, such as personality or in this case to hormonal factors. We could also attribute to causes external to the person, such as the situation the person is in. So we could attribute a person's mood to external stress, the way they are being treated and so on. What are the effects of attributing Mrs. Brown's behavior to hormones (an internal cause)? What are the potential disadvantages, limitations, or harmful outcomes of attributing too much to biology?

4. Can you think of examples of others making attributions about you; or you making them about others, where the accuracy of the attributions later turned out to be questionnable?

4.

STICKS OR CARROTS?

Elinore and I were grocery shopping. Just before we got to the ice cream aisle, we heard high-pitched screeching. Rounding the stacks of cereals, we gained a view of the ice cream freezers. It only took a few seconds to take in the scene. Harried young mom pushing loaded cart with an infant; other child, a boy about four years old who was screaming and reaching for ice cream. Mom attempting to prevent infant from falling while restraining boy from reaching freezer. She was saying "NO" to him while he took turns kicking at her and swinging at her arms as she tried to control him.

I took a quick look around. Most shoppers were carefully ignoring the scene. Not Elinore though, she headed straight for the besieged woman. "I will take care of your little one. You deal with the boy", she said. Elinore picked the infant up and began talking to her and bouncing her. Meanwhile, the mom went to the boy and they had a tussle. She grabbed an arm and tried to pull him away from the ice cream. He flopped down on the floor; tears rolling down his cheeks, arms rigidly flailing the ground, screeching at full volume.

I was curious to see how this little drama would play out. Mom was holding firm. Not giving in to the boy. It must have been hugely embarrassing for her to have this scene witnessed by so many. If I had been in her position, I would have wondered what the other shoppers would think of my mothering skills. Would they think I was a bad mother for having such an unruly child?

However, she kept talking to the boy and eventually they ended up putting a small box of ice cream into the cart. As they headed to the check-out, with Elinore still carrying the little one, I picked up our ice cream. The boy was quieter and Elinore and the mom were chatting.

As we parted after leaving the store, Elinore filled me in. "That was Helen. She is temporarily a single parent while her husband is away with the military for several months. She has no family in this area. I told her to drop Devon off with us tomorrow afternoon while she takes a nap with the little one." My mouth must have hung open. I knew Elinore tried to be helpful, but babysitting Devon seemed a bit much. Elinore caught my look, "Helen has her hands full. She doesn't feel she can manage Devon's behavior. The relationship between Helen and Devon is on a bad track. I want to help."

Helen dropped Devon off the next afternoon. He was in a good mood until we came inside. "Hungry" he grunted, looking at the fridge.

"I asked Helen not to feed him lunch before bringing him over. A hungry child is a motivated child", Elinore said to me with a knowing smile. Meanwhile, Devon not seeing any response, headed for the fridge. He opened for the freezer compartment spotting the ice cream carton, but not quite able to reach it.

"Ice cream....give me...want it" Devon got straight to the point.

"Would you like me to give you some ice cream?" Elinore asked.

"Want it.. give me" Devon was becoming agitated reaching for it and starting to whine.

"Sit here" said Elinore, pushing a chair to the table and placing a red bowl on the table.

Devon stopped whining and looked at the bowl. Elinore got a spoon out of the drawer and made a big show of placing it next to the bowl. "Sit here" she repeated. He jumped on the chair. "Good boy" she said. "Ice cream is coming." She went to the freezer and with a great flourish started scooping. "I like the way you are waiting" she said as Devon was sitting surprisingly quietly in anticipation. Finally, she brought what she had dug out of the freezer. I was amazed to see that the amount that she placed in the bowl was about half a tablespoon, a tiny amount. Devon gobbled it greedily. He then held up his bowl to show that it was empty.

"More" he said.

"Would you like me to give you more ice cream?" Elinore asked, hovering by the freezer, scooping spoon suggestively in her hand.

"More!" he said.

Elinore scooped some out. It took a little longer this time. I was beginning to glimpse her plan. She was having him wait quietly a bit longer each time. Again it was a tiny amount that she gave him.

"More" he said in a few seconds.

"Say 'please'" responded Elinore. Devon just fussed and started to whine.

"More, want more, give me" he continued increasingly demanding and agitated in a whinny way.

I noticed that Elinore made a point of not paying attention to Devon when he behaved badly. I was surprised to see that when he started to get upset, Elinore immediately stopped talking to him, and even stepped away from the fridge. As soon as Devon paused the bad behavior, Elinore got into action talking to him, moving to the ice cream, and flourishing her scooping spoon.

This was the opposite of what I thought would be most people's natural reaction, which would be to pay attention and comfort when the child was upset (and behaving badly). Elinore told me later that she deliberately was not going to reinforce the bad behavior such as whining and tantrumming. She was determinedly and planfully only going to reinforcing the desirable behaviors (such as waiting calmly, asking politely) rather than either punishing or rewarding the undesirable.

I understood Elinore's strategy. It did seem a lot of work, though. "Why not just punish him when he is badly behaved? Wouldn't that get straight to the point?" I asked.

"The problem with punishment is that people think that it works simply. Sometimes it does work in a direct way but punishment is far less predictable than most people think it is" she replied. "There are many issues", she continued. "For example, parents and teachers often give punishment when they're angry. So they're not precisely punishing a specific behavior; they are punishing the child. To the child, the punishing person seems angry and threatening. The child often responds with anxiety, fear, or anger. Often, the child's goal becomes not to do the desired behavior but to just avoid punishment and the punisher.

Punishment by itself is not informative, it does not tell the child what is the desired response. The child whines, gets punished. Does that tell the child he is supposed to wait quietly the next time? It still surprises me when people punish children and expect to magically get good behavior."

"The best strategy is to reward good behavior and try to ignore the bad", she said definitively.

"Why do some kids develop obnoxiously bad behavior?" I asked, while Elinore continued to get calmer, more polite and longer waiting behaviors from Devon which were rewarded with tiny portions of ice cream.

"I think bad behavior is often established because busy or overwhelmed parents inadvertently pay more attention when the kids are bad, and less attention to them when they are not causing trouble. Guess what they end up reinforcing? Its tragic, really." She shook her head.

I started to think about behavior from the perspective of this kind of analysis. An idea flashed in my mind. "Elinore, so what happens when parents try to not reinforce tantrums, like Helen initially tried to do in the store." I was trying to get my thoughts straight, "but then sometimes eventually give in, that can't be good", I ended up not being able to express my thoughts exactly.

"You are on track" Elinore replied enthusiastically, "keep with that thought."

It then clicked for me, "they are putting the kid on a variable ratio schedule of reinforcement for tantrumming."

"Exactly, and you know how resistant to extinction that schedule makes behavior" Elinore concluded my thoughts.

"So why do parents give in?" I asked.

"They are negatively reinforced in the short run. The tantrum stops. By giving in to the tantrum, the parents terminate the tantrum, which was a very unpleasant stimulus," Elinore explained. "By the way, I don't want you mixing up the terms 'punishment' and 'negative reinforcement'. Many people have trouble with this.

Negative reinforcement is not an easy concept. An organism is negatively reinforced when its behavior results in the removal of an unpleasant stimulus." She came up with another example. "Suppose you have a headache. You take two aspirins. The headache goes away. Your behavior of taking the aspirin is negatively reinforced by the removal of the headache."

"I get it", I said, even though I was still not sure if I did.

I left Elinore and Devon as she patiently continued to get him small bits of ice cream as a reward for good behavior. He left in a good mood. Elinore explained to Helen what she had done.

I thought we were finished with Devon, but a few days later Helen called. She was practicing reinforcing good behavior and ignoring the bad but a different problem had come up. Devon had developed many cavities. His first visit to the dentist had resulted in some pain. The attempted second visit had to be postponed because Devon had become so anxious and fearful at the dentist that no work could be accomplished.

I went along for Devon's next visit to the dentist. Even before getting to the office, Devon started to cry and complain. Once we got in the door he started to tremble. His breathing became rapid and shallow. He tried to head for the door. I lunged for him and held onto him. He was sweating and I could feel his tiny heart racing as I held onto him. He was in panic mode and no attempts to talk him down worked. Nothing was going to get him into the dentist's chair. He actually threw up in the car on the way home.

Later, I described this to Elinore. I ended up by letting her know that I did not feel Devon was 'acting', he was feeling genuine terror. His behavior was different than at the store. "What do you think was going on?" I asked Elinore.

"Does the name Pavlov ring a bell?" she asked me jokingly. She continued without waiting for an answer. "What you saw sounds like a classically conditioned response. It comes about through the association of stimuli. The dental office and pain have been paired together. Now the dental office alone, even without pain, brings about the response of fear, trembling, and anxiety. It is the same response that the actual pain elicits. It is not voluntary."

"You are right, Mariah, this is different than the behavior we saw in the ice-cream tantrum. That behavior was determined by its consequences. If Devon gets what he wants by tantrumming, he will continue to do so. If he is not rewarded for the tantrums, the behavior will eventually extinguish, that is stop."

"What can be done for the classically conditioned anxiety?" I wanted to know.

"I can tell you what to do but doing it might be difficult, she said."

"Tell me" I asked.

"Fear is based on pain, anticipated pain, uncertainty, lack of knowledge, loss of control. Devon's fears may be reduced if he knows more about what goes on in the dental office. Make an appointment with the dental assistant. Go on a visit with Devon, letting him know that no work will be performed on him that day. Show him around, let him ask questions, have him sit in the dental chair, and maybe show him a picture book about teeth. Have him study his own teeth with a mirror. Get him feeling knowledgeable, comfortable. Take him out for a fun activity afterwards. Keep talking about teeth, all the while making sure he is fairly relaxed. Get some calm, positive, and pleasant association to dentistry for him. Praise him for progress."

It was time for dinner. Delicious smells from the kitchen triggering my conditioned response of hunger and salivation, I tried to experiment with stopping those responses. I was not very successful. I gained some sympathy for Devon. It is probably just as hard for him to control his conditioned anxiety as it is for me to control salivation when hungry and smelling delicious aromas.

As we sat down for dinner Elinore poured herself a very large glass of wine. She sighed. "It is not too late to help Devon, but I am frustrated with what is happening in with Joanna."

I did not quite get the connection so I said, "fill me in".

She sighed again, "as far as I can tell, the main lesson that Joanna learned as a child was that she would be punished for any instance of non-compliance. The related lesson that she learned was that if you want to keep someone's love and approval then you must do and say what that person wants. Her father was a strong believer in using punishment. He sounds like he was the power in the family and he parented in an angry and demanding manner."

Elinor refilled her wine glass. I took the pause in her words to ask for clarification. "What is the connection between Devon and Joanna?"

"Both their behaviors can be understood in terms of how they have been reinforced and punished", Elinore answered. I was not sure if I understood but Elinore continued.

"If Joanna acted differently than what her father wanted, he saw that as defiance. He would punish her. Threats, hits, yelling, withdrawal of approval and love, these were his tactics. Apparently he had conditioned Joanna's mother to be compliant as well. So Joanna had no models in childhood of how to be an individual, especially in relation to a man. Even now, years later, just thinking about not pleasing someone she has a relationship with, makes her feel uncomfortable and vaguely anxious."

"My thought is that as a child she was strongly punished for any act of non-compliance. She is completely geared to avoiding punishment by trying to understand what others want and then to meet those expectations. Sometimes she does not even have any idea of what she wants. Mariah, even in her sessions with me, she is looking to figure out what I want for her and trying to comply. Of course, what I want is for her to be independent! That's an unfamiliar and scary sensation for her. Without thinking about it, she is comfortable with a man similar to her father. With such a man she can take the familiar compliant role, and that is something she knows she can do well."

"Worst of all, she has re-contacted the man that she was previously involved with and is considering going back to live with him." Elinore sighed again. "Joanna is still responding in the ways she learned as a child from the way she was reinforced and punished."

"At first, in her relationship with her boyfriend, she received lots of positive reinforcement. Attention, compliments, flattery, flowers, dinners, intimacy. For Joanna, who had in the past been so short of this kind of reinforcement, the initial stage of the relationship was wonderful. She bonded to the guy."

"As time went on, his reinforcement came less often. He made other priorities for himself, he paid her less attention, less often. You would expect that Joanna would also cool to him, but surprisingly the opposite happened. Why? Look at what she is going through in terms of schedules of reinforcement. At the beginning of the relationship, she smiles at her guy, talks to him, cooks for him; he responds positively nearly every time. She is on a near continuous schedule of reinforcement; that is she does something, he reinforces almost each time.

Later, though she is on a variable ratio reinforcement schedule. She does nice things for him; he responds in a reinforcing way less and less often. She never knows when he will be attentive and kind to her. We know from laboratory experiments that rats put on this kind of schedule work harder and harder to get the reinforcer and their behavior is extremely resistant to extinction. Some rats will literally work themselves to death on a variable ratio reinforcement schedule."

"This is the sad thing. Had Joanna been with a dependable fellow who provided predictable reinforcement, she would probably be content. If that kind of man stopped being reinforcing she would quickly realize the relationship was over and move on. In a continuous reinforcement schedule the stopping of reinforcement leads to rapid extinction of the behavior. In this case the behavior of Joanna working to maintain the relationship would rapidly extinguish. But with this variable ratio schedule, she just keeps on trying to maintain the relationship and tries to get the reinforcement of his attention and approval. It is as if once used to getting reinforced on a near random basis, she just does not know when to quit trying; her effort at maintaining the relationship is never extinguished."

This way of thinking was completely new to me. I had always thought that people who stayed in bad relationships or were indecisive had to have low self-esteem or be lacking in will power. Elinore was encouraging me to think about their behavior in terms of past and current punishment and reinforcement. It was a different perspective.

Elinore concluded the chat, "I wish Joanna could find something other than this relationship that would give her the reinforcement that she needs. Other friendships, work, study, hobbies, anything might do; although of course it is hard to find an activity that is potentially as reinforcing as a good intimate relationship."

---

1. What happens when you are punished or threatened with punishment? How has punishment worked on you? How about reinforcement?

2.Think of some real life examples of the use of punishment with children. Are alternatives available in these instances?

3. Can you think of instances where bad adult or child behavior is inadvertently reinforced?

4. Can you think of real life examples of various schedules of reinforcement?

5. Can you list some of your classically conditioned responses? (perhaps to certain foods, people, places, music, sounds).

6. Do you intentionally manage your responses to other peoples' behavior so you can be reinforcing or punishing?

7. Can you think of ways in which your own history of reinforcement has influenced you?

5.

Those Doggone Memories

Elinore and I are dealing with children again. The girls in this case were referred after attempts to resolve which parent should get custody of them after the marriage broke down. However, right from the start I knew this case was going to be intense and there might be no neat resolution, as there had been with Tom. The strategy for dealing with this situation is that I interview and observe. Later, Elinore will debrief me and we will discuss.

Session 1, Ellen and Kathy.

Ellen is barely 12 but she is acting like a fiercely protective parent. Whenever I ask for clarification of her sister Kathy's story, Ellen interprets it as a threat to Kathy and reacts with counterattack. Her eyes flash at me with the ferocity of a mother tiger whose kitten is being threatened. She angrily yells, "Don't you believe her?" She turns repeatedly from Kathy to me. Her straight, shoulder length dark hair swings like a matador's cape with each turn, covering and uncovering her eyes. She is daring me to look her in the eye and say I doubt her sister. There is determination in every line of her face. "I thought you were supposed to help us," she says in a tone that is as direct and confrontational as the eyes.

Kathy, is the younger sister. She is nine years old. Her thumb wanders to her mouth, is sucked for a few moments, is spat out. Seconds later the thumb returns and the cycle repeats. Although physically the same size as her sister, she is operating on a far younger emotional level. Her shoulders shake and her voice is shrill. She is telling me her story. It seems that she is fully re-experiencing the events as she is talking. She is demonstrating sexual assaults that she says her father did to her. She puts her hand near her crotch area and moves it in a vigorous and exaggerated rubbing motion. The facial muscles are contorted. She is distressed. I fear she is near a breakdown. I half expect her to just close down, curl into a crying ball, and shut everyone out. That is not what happens. Instead she goes on, repeating her story. Her distress gradually morphs into anger. Anger and even hate of her father, David.

Kathy's emotions are real. She is not acting. But there are bits that do not fit. In the midst of the serious sexual abuse allegations she goes on, "and he massaged my back when it hurt, and he touched my knee in the car, and he picked me up by the armpits, and he put lotion on my neck when I got that sunburn". These statements are said with the exact same vehemence and disgust as the serious allegations. Due to Ellen's interference, I can't ask clarification about these "touchings". There is more, "and he made me stand in the corner in my pajamas when Ellen and I were giggling after bedtime; and dad made Ranger go in the basement for an hour after she peed on the living room rug. Dad is always so mean."

A recurring theme was about the family dog, Ranger. "She used to be gentle and kind," said Ellen. "She took care of us and we loved her," added Kathy. Then Ranger got sick according to the girls. She would bark and howl for no reason. She started to growl and snap, even at the girls. David locked her in the shed. However, Ranger got no better. She became even more scary. Near the end, she was crazed and frothing at the mouth.

One day David asked the girls to say goodbye to her. Then he left the house for the shed with his shotgun. In a while they heard a shot and never saw Ranger again. They had not talked of this to anyone. "Mom loves all creatures, David hates animals," they explained. The memories of the dog were confused. All this must have happened very long ago; I think when they were preschoolers.

I was confused by the 'piling on'. A few horrendous incidents would probably have convinced me. Why add information about the dog peeing on the rug? I suppose a back massage or putting lotion on the neck could easily have sexual overtones but Ellen and Kathy seemed to believe these 'touchings' were obviously and always wrong in and of themselves. Where would they acquire that concept? Also, the forceful statements, the repetition, the anger, all did not fit what Elinore had told me to expect. "Usually, the predominant emotions in a disclosure of abuse are shame, fear and hesitation," she had said. I was getting only anger.

I wondered, who needed to be convinced of the awfulness of dad and why? And why was I questioning their story? What if he truly had done those awful things? How could I live with myself for doubting these girls for a minute?

Session 2, Dad.

Elinore and I met the father together. David seemed to be in disbelief of his own story even while he was telling it. Life had been normal until the marital separation three years ago. He had loved Ellen and Kathy and they had loved him. Although he worked long hours and the mother had done most of the parenting in the early years, there had been good father-daughter times.

Holidays to Disneyland, camping trips, and pets. He listed them off and dropped photos on the coffee table. Pictures of a pair of happy looking girls. Dozens of pictures of the smiling girls; including some very old ones with Ranger. The most recent picture with Ranger showed Ellen as about 4 or 5 years old. It was not reasonable that Kathy, who was only 2 or 3 years old at the last picture with Ranger could have detailed memories of her own. She could only be recalling what others had told her more recently. I got the feeling that the photos were presented to reassure David, Elinore and I that once there had been closeness and happiness.

Now there was an unbridgeable distance between the girls and him. His voice broke as he continued the story. After the separation, the girls came to his house every second weekend. The rest of their time was with Mom. His perception was that Mom became critical of him. She did not miss any opportunity to show her dislike and distrust for him in front of the girls. On each occasion that he picked them up for the weekend, mom let the girls know that she did not trust him. In front of him she would say to the girls things like, "I don't like it but the Judge said you have to spend the weekend with him"; "David and the Judge don't know how girls feel, but I do"; "If he hurts you, phone me and I will come get you right away"; "when you feel bad, just remember you will be back with Mom soon and I will make it better."

After a few weeks of this he noticed that the girls were anxious and apprehensive when he came to mom's door for the weekend pick-up. They were only nine and six years old then. They would cling to mom and sometimes he would have to literally pull them away from her. Then mom would say to the girls, "When I lived with him he used to force me to do things I hated, too." David said he detested these scenes and even wondered whether he should stop seeing the girls to save them from conflict. But he came to the decision that the girls needed to know their father and that he needed a relationship with them.

When he returned the girls to mother, another drama would take place. She would come out onto the porch of her house, place herself between the girls and him, turn her back to him, physically turn the girls away from him. She would squat down, an arm around the back of each child, all three turned away from him and toward her door. She was acting like a mother hen, using her arms like wings to protect her chicks from a predator. No acknowledgement of him; he might as well have been invisible. Then, "I was so worried about you with him; I get sick when I think of you two alone with him; at least he brought you back this time; now tell me what he did to you" This last said as they disappeared through her door.

David said battles about custody and visitation had raged on over the next three years. It was expensive, stressful, and nothing got resolved. In fact, he noticed that the more time they spent battling, the more bitter and extreme the conflict between him and the mother became. Just when it seemed that things could not get worse, they got much worse. Kathy told her maternal grandmother that David had been sexually abusing her. An initial investigation by a social worker indicated that the girls' stories corroborated each other and the girls were clearly terrified of their father. The worker indicated that Kathy "visibly cringed" at mention of the possibility of spending another weekend with David.

"This is a horrible mess," Elinore said after David had left. "I am not sure if there is any way to help these poor girls. You talk to mom. We will see if we have any bright ideas after that."

Session 3, Mom.

This case was really disturbing to me. I was not sleeping well. In the morning I was off to see the mom. Vicki greeted me warmly on her porch and sat me down and brought some lemonade out. She was an outgoing, attractive woman. I asked her about Kathy's disclosure. Grandma had always been suspicious of David, she informed me. Grandma had been on a rare visit from New York. The disclosure had begun a huge family commotion, and soon all the relatives had the story repeated for them by Kathy and Ellen. Neighbors, too, had come over. Everyone got involved. The support given to her and the girls was magnificent. People wanted her to never return the girls to David. They were willing to write letters of support to the Courts.

Vicki told me that she had met David when they both had been traveling. She thought he was a sophisticated and ambitious man. Ellen was born a year after their marriage. Kathy, three years later. He missed both childbirths because he was at work. Him not being present at the births really bothered her. It was her first sign that he did not care about family.

After children, she had become increasingly disappointed in him. He had not changed diapers, cleaned or cooked. He worked long hours and paid little or no attention to the "three women". When he was home, he slept, watched TV, or read the paper. Vicki had a love of animals and she always had pets for the girls but David always ignored animals and felt them to be a bother.

Vicki said she began to realize that his disinterest and intolerance of animals was just a reflection of his uncaring nature to every living thing (including her and the girls). She was always taking in stray and injured animals; he was always trying to get them out of the house. Vicki felt she was showing love and compassion; she felt he was demonstrating selfishness to the girls. Vicki felt she was in fact a 'single parent' and had to assume sole responsibility for the girls as she saw his influence as being negative. She increasingly came to see him as mean and selfish. She did not want a man like this influencing her precious girls. The marital relationship deteriorated. Communication ceased. Eventually she asked for the divorce.

After the separation, she said she was stunned to find out that David wanted the girls half the time. "He never did anything with them before, why would he want to start now?" she asked me angrily. Her misgivings increased as the girls reported back after the weekend visits that he did obtain through a Court order. He had not cooked meals but took them to fast food places. Sometimes he dropped them off at one of these places and did some errands. One time he was an hour late coming back. Another time the girls sat in the car for an hour and a half in the driveway of a client, while David did business with the man inside the house. The last straw was a weekend when Ellen returned to her with an untreated fever and Kathy had unexplained bruises on her spine. These were a series of round, equal sized bruises, up and down her spine. Vicki could not think of an accidental way this could have occurred. Suspecting abuse, she asked David about it. He had told her he had no idea of how this had happened and showed no interest or concern.

She was terrified of having the girls neglected or hurt by David. She wanted to find out what was actually occurring on the visits. So Vicki did question the girls upon their return. She also wanted to encourage the girls to have the strength to stand up to what she saw as David's inconsideration and neglect, so she would coach them before visits on what they could say and do if he became seriously disrespectful or negligent of them.

Another thing that annoyed Vicki was how David spent time with the girls. She said, "He was always dragging them along to do what he wanted to do." In contrast she said, "I think about their needs, their choices. I have always wanted them to grow up to be strong and caring women. Ever since they were little, I have wanted to nurture these traits. The best way to do this when they are young is to have them taking care of animals. So I have always encouraged pets, going to animal shelters and taking on different care-taking roles. David had no time for that. He made us move into town when Ellen was five years old and we had to get rid of several animals then. He even hated it when the girls and I would watch those wonderful old Disney movies that starred animals."

I could see that Vicki was exceptionally sympathetic to animals. I wondered why she had not brought up the tragic end of Ranger. How could she continue with him as a partner or father after that? It must have been a major turning point in her feelings about David, and the more I thought about it the more curious I was about why she had not mentioned it. Too painful?

I had a more urgent line to explore with her. Yesterday, when I had talked about this upcoming visit with Vicki, Elinore had been helpful. She had said, "Lets assume both parents want what is best for the kids. Also lets assume that neither one is crazy nor abusive. Nearly all parents try very hard to do good for their kids. How could this impossible mess have come about?" She then came up with some possible ideas.

"Lets take Vicki's perspective first. We know Vicki is anxious about David's parenting. She thinks he won't pay attention to the girls, won't listen to them, probably neglect them, and make them feel like insignificant pawns in his life. Possibly, Vicki herself has had similar painful experiences with men. She is determined not to let this happen to her girls. So she prepares them for the outings with David. In the preparation she inadvertently conveys the message that she expects David to be mean, uncaring, insensitive and generally nasty."

"Now lets look at this from the girls' view. They sense that mom is anxious and tense about David. Her fear rises as the time for him to pick them up comes closer. They are shoved in the middle of this tension. Their primary caregiver, the person they are emotionally close to, the person they are gender identified with, the person they depend upon the most can't help but communicate that David is a bad person. How are the girls going to interpret anything he does? What chance does he have? If he gives a massage will that be seen as a kind act or an awkward and uncomfortable one? How much suspicion will they have toward him? How will these expectations color their reactions?"

"Then the girls return to mom. They have spent a tense weekend. They are relieved to see mom. Mom is relieved to see them. Thus the departure of David is associated with renewed mother-daughter bonding and easing of tension. Everyone feels better when he is gone. Vicki questions the girls. They know she expects to hear bad stuff. They have already interpreted whatever has happened with David in the worst possible way. There is a need for consensus and bonding among the three after their anxious separation and it will readily come from a shared perspective about David. They will be motivated to stand together against him. They will reinforce each other for seeing him negatively."

"Last, we come to David. In his mind, mom is deliberately turning the girls against him. The girls act in a cynical and cruel manner to him. He gets frustrated. He might think, 'they are just like Vicki'. His reaction to them would then come from a helpless and stressed place. He might assert his authority and exert discipline to try to prevent them from being 'like Vicki'. The girls would perceive him as mean. In reaction, their behavior would become more difficult. You can play out the cycle."

With this perspective from Elinore in the back of my mind, I said to Vicki, "Do you think it is possible, just possible, that the girls negative reaction to David is in part a reflection of your feelings about him?"

"What could you possibly mean?" she snapped at me. "He has molested Kathy. I would say he has done plenty to earn their resentment all on his own." She was furious with me. I had to give it one more push. "Do you really believe he sexually abused her?" She backed off from the instant rage reaction that I was expecting. She thought for a while. Finally, she barked, "I will tell you. Nothing David does surprises me anymore. He will never be alone with them again. I don't care if he did it. Kathy saying it is enough for me. Even if he didn't do it, she must have a strong reason for saying it happened. That's good enough for me. I am glad she is asserting herself. Standing up for herself is the main thing. Who cares if he did it?" With that she turned away from me and went into the house. I was left alone on the porch holding the dregs of my lemonade. I realized the interview was over. I had again forgotten to ask about Ranger.

Session 4, home visit.

The following Saturday, I am over at David's house. At Elinore's suggestion, I am supervising a visit of the girls with David. Supervision means that there has to be an adult, besides David present. The adult is me. Elinore thought I might be able to make some helpful observations. I come prepared to do some baking with the girls. David has planned no activities. I take the baking stuff out. The girls join in enthusiastically. We are having a great time and David actually joins in to help. The phone rings. Vicki calling for Kathy. To my astonishment, immediately as Kathy begins speaking her demeanor changes. Lowering her voice into the phone, she says, "Mom, I'm so scared, I want to go home, I don't know what to do." After a little more whispered conversation, she hangs up the phone and another immediate change in her demeanor, that of a happy child about to bake cookies, took place.

The girls are off to clean up after the baking. I take David aside to ask him about Ranger. Elinore had said that shooting the dog verges on the sadistic. We had to figure out what why he did it. "Haven't seen her in years", he says, yawning in response to my "tell me about Ranger".

"Of course not," I say, "but why did you choose to kill her that way?"

He becomes more alert, "kill?"

"Yes, the girls say you shot her when she was sick".

He is fully alert now. "Last I heard, Ranger was alive and well at my friend Bill's place," he says. "Could not keep her in the apartment we were moving to, so I found a real nice place for her." I try not to let my jaw hang too loose.

While I am trying to absorb this bit of news I remember to ask him about Kathy's spinal bruises from years back. He surprises me by saying, "Vicki noticed them first. I could not figure out where they came from at the time Vicki asked. Next time the girls came over I figured it out. Kathy had been trying to learn to bicycle. She would pedal a few feet, get the bike moving at a good clip, then get scared. She had not learned use the brakes so stopped by moving forward off the seat and putting both feet on the ground. She stopped but the momentum of the bike meant that the front of the bike seat hit her in the lower back. Caused a bunch of round bruises. Didn't seem to bother her." I silently thought to myself, 'and you could not be bothered to tell Vicki once you figured it out.'

Session 5, consultation with Elinore.

I reported on the visit and what David had said about Ranger. The darned dog was getting increasingly important. Elinore said that what happened when Mom phoned Kathy was confirmation of her initial hunch. Elinore thought that the phone observation was the key one that I had made. These girls can't tell mom they are having a good time with dad; in fact they stop having a good time as soon as they realize they are not feeling bad. Not that dad is a great parent.

The news about Ranger was another key. Assuming the dog is really alive, how could the girls have the memories of her being sick and getting shot?

The phone rang. I picked it up. It was the vet's office reminding Elinore that it was time for her dog's rabies shot. I told Elinore. She said nothing but froze like a statue. Then her hands and face started moving. I watched as ideas bubbled inside her. Finally, she said to me, "Phone Vicki and see if the girls ever saw an old Disney movie called 'Old Yeller'". In confusion I did so. Vicki informed me that it was their favorite film, and the girls saw it several times when they were very young but had not seen it in at least six years.

Elinore was excited, she was talking to herself but increasingly loudly, "rabies, rabies, RABIES, RABIES, beloved dog, mad and aggressive behavior by dog, out of character behavior by dog, dog needs to be killed, is shot out of sight, but the shot is heard, this is straight out of the classic Disney movie 'Old Yeller'," she said.

She turned to me, "I think these girls memories of the movie 'Old Yeller' got mixed up and confabulated with their memories of Ranger and his absence. One day Ranger was there, then gone. They saw the movie and years later, the two separate stories just got stuck into one. I can easily imagine a bitter Vicki saying to the girls something like, 'that's exactly what your father would have done to a sick animal.'"

Final consultation with Elinor.

Yesterday, I had watched as the girls met Ranger after seven years absence. Ranger had been joyous. The girls had been initially hesitant, then confused, and finally happy. Bravely they had acknowledged that it really was Ranger.

Then we watched 'Old Yeller' together. It exactly matched what they thought David had done to Ranger. The girls had faced the truly horrifying idea that what they thought they knew for certain, clearly remembered, and believed with all their hearts, was not true.

Elinore explained that we are all subject to the kinds of distortions that had happened to the girls' memories. There is no fixed videotape in our heads. We construct memories each time we recall an event. The girls knew that David did not like animals and was not kind to them. Vicki supported their beliefs about David being insensitive and cruel to animals. Ranger had disappeared from their lives. The dog in the movie and Ranger were physically similar. It might have taken only the slightest possibly unintentional suggestion from Vicki, to start their thoughts on the parallel between Ranger's fate and the fate of 'Old Yeller' in the movie.

Elinore said she hesitated momentarily before recommending that the girls meet Ranger. On the one hand, she felt it was extremely harsh to demonstrate to the girls that their memories could sometimes be in error. This step could make them question everything about their pasts and make them doubt themselves, possibly excessively. On the other hand, it wasn't right to have the girls believe that David had killed the dog, when he hadn't.

Elinore was just as concerned about the sexual abuse recollections. "Are they false or accurate?" she wondered. "How would we ever know? How would these girls have a sense of their parents now that they know the accuracy of their memories is questionable. You know, we accept that we forget events; why is it so hard to accept that we might remember things that never happened?"

The requirement is for about a 500 word response to this assignment. The main issue has to do with the reconstructive nature of memory. At any point time we construct our memories from all the available information. This includes material gathered since the events that originally led to the memory.

There is no unchangeable hard drive in the brain. Factors that can lead to transformation of the original memory include: misinformation, suggestion, imaginarily going over the memory, confounding several events, and corroboration of the erroneous memory by another person (as the sisters did for each other here). You might want to detail how the false memories about the dog could have come about. What are the factors that may have contributed? Did the failure of the parents to communicate with each other contribute? Did the perception that each parent had of the other promote these false memories? How? Similar experiences may be included.

The fable is meant to illustrate that memory is subject to many forces. Nothing in this fable is meant to imply that people's traumatic memories are generally false.

6.

COMMUNICATION CONFUSION

I returned from a long jog and found Elinore pouring tea for Dr. Brown and two other people I had not previously met. One was a guy named Malcolm. As I was introduced to him, I noticed his wonderfully clear blue eyes. The other person was a woman. Her name was Lisa. Elinore looked directly at Dr. Brown. "How can we help?" she inquired.

Dr. Brown told his story with a worried frown on his face. There had been several instances of attempted or borderline sexual assaults on campus. No woman had been physically hurt but there had been serious upset and emotional damage.

Dr. Brown had prepared a plan of action. He had briefed a counselor. A seminar had been prepared for the male students. The seminar was to cover issues such as respecting women's wishes; the right of individuals to say 'no'; the responsibility to listen to the 'no'; date rape; and so on. Dr. Brown was pleased with the proposed seminar and had hoped that it would resolve the problems.

He was therefore surprised, when just prior to the scheduled seminar, several men approached the counselor and blamed these incidents on the behavior of the women students, saying the women had been the ones to initiate intimate contact and then later changed their minds prior to actual intercourse. It was the women, not the men, they claimed who had been more aggressive.

Dr. Brown asked, "How is it possible for two people to both see the other as more sexually forward and aggressive than they see themselves?" He wanted to know if Elinore had any suggestions.

Elinore seemed to be thinking and the silence was broken by Malcolm "possibly these guys are just trying to deflect the blame."

"I think there is more to it," said Dr. Brown, "the counselor felt the men were being sincere."

After a pause, Dr. Brown looked at Lisa. "Lisa was involved in one of these incidents. Perhaps she could give us more information."

Lisa looked distinctly uncomfortable. I could see this was going to be difficult for her. I made a decision. "Lisa, if you would come with me I could get the details while the others get on with making plans." She cast me a look of relief and accompanied me to the kitchen.

When we were alone, she started. "We were just getting to know each other, you know. Just having fun. Nothing serious. He was really cute, interesting, nice. Then all of a sudden wham. His hands were in places they should not have been. I mean it was like so fast."

"Back up a bit", I said. "How did you meet, what were you doing?"

"We knew each other from one class we had together. We had studied together several times. One evening after studying, he walked me home. He was fun. My roommate was out. I complained of a sore neck. He offered to give me a neck and shoulder massage. To make it more comfortable I changed into my pajamas. He started to massage my shoulders. It felt good. Then wham, his hands were all over me and he pushed me down onto the couch and got on top of me with all his weight. He dug his fingers into my arms. He bruised me. Want to see?"

Without waiting she pulled her sleeves up, revealing finger-sized ugly purple circles on her upper arms.

"What happened then?" I asked.

"He tried to rip my pajamas off. It was awful. I yelled at him to stop, he wouldn't. After about the third time I screamed at him to stop, I could see I got through to him. He got an angry look. As he got off me, he gripped my arms and bruised me. He didn't say anything, not even an apology. Just walked away with a mad look", she finished visibly upset. But not quite finished, "I have not gone to that class since. I could not bear to see him, at least until he apologizes."

We rejoined the others. "I have brought Malcolm along as I would like a male perspective on this as well", Dr. Brown said. I was not fully listening to him as I kept noticing that Malcolm had those lovely blue eyes. He moved gracefully. He was very attractive.

To my surprise, without first asking me, Elinore agreed with Dr. Brown, "I think it is a good idea to have a team approach to this task. Will that work for you, Mariah?"

Without waiting for my answer Malcolm took charge. "I see you have talked to Lisa. I will interview the guy, Steve. After I have obtained the information from him, you and I will get together and compare notes. Malcolm was very direct and once again did not wait for my response.

However, Dr. Brown and Lisa took this as the cue for all to leave. There was an awkward moment as Malcolm went out the door. He left going out backwards and almost tripped. I could not tell if he was trying to get one final glance at me, or what he was trying to do.

The next night, Malcolm and I sat together in Elinore's living room. "I have interviewed Steve", he reported. "Steve was led on by Lisa. Lisa invited him over; she knew that her roommate would be out and they would be alone; she invited him to touch her with the neck massage; and she changed her clothes for pajamas. I can't see any possible reason why Steve would be at fault on this", he said with an air of finality.

I felt that this was a rush to judgment. He had not asked about what Lisa had said to me. I touched him on the arm to get him to pay attention to me. "Look at this from Lisa's perspective. There was no discussion about the two of them having a close relationship; there was no discussion of having sex; there was no building of any kind of close intimacy. He gave no verbal indication that he was interested in having sex with her any time, no indication that he had that idea that evening, yet he physically started to have sex with her. How could he possibly think he had her consent?"

Malcolm looked over at me with a puzzled expression.

I continued, "Do you think that a specific behavior such as putting on the pajamas; or a massage; or even being alone privately could have meant something completely different to Lisa and to Steve? That is they took completely different meanings and implications from these actions?" I asked him.

Didn't appear that he had thought of that possibility and he was not going to give up easily. "What could Lisa have possibly been thinking? She did admit she liked Steve."

"Well, lets see", I started, "she could have thought that inviting him over could be a way of getting to know each other better; that getting a massage would be way of getting closer in a nonsexual way; that putting on pajamas would show that she trusted him and could be comfortable being casual with him.

Liking him and wanting to sleep with him might be different things."

Malcolm seemed to be actually listening to me and thinking about what I had said. He sat quietly for a while. "I never thought that some men and some women might think so differently about the process of making a close relationship", Malcolm admitted. I admired his honesty. I was even more pleased that instead of making decisions on his own, Malcolm had respected my thoughts.

"Hey, what would you think about you going to see Steve and explaining to him that there might have been some miscommunication between him and Lisa. I will talk to Lisa. Maybe, we can bring the two of them together and help them feel better about each other and learn something from this episode?" I asked Malcolm. We agreed to do that the next day. We had a pleasant chat before he left. I walked him to the door. As he left he ended up going out the door backwards, awkwardly. This was the second time I had seen him do that.

Malcolm and I met the next evening to debrief at a campus restaurant. It had been his suggestion. I dressed for the occasion as if it was a date. He looked good, too. However, neither of us had success with Lisa and Steve. We had explained that there had been a misunderstanding between them; that cues and behaviors had been interpreted differently than intended; and that neither planned to intentionally mislead or assault. However, each of them was still anxious and angry at the other. Lisa said she was frightened of Steve and was physically ill at even the thought of seeing him. Steve was angry and bitter about what had happened to his reputation and refused to see Lisa unless she first publicly cleared him. (Lisa had been sobbing when her roommate came home that night, the roommate had told others, the story had spread).

Malcolm and I had a pleasant talk over dinner about our future school plans. I also talked about my family but he didn't pick up the cue and said nothing about his family. In fact, he seemed a bit fidgety when family came up in the conversation. In a pause in the conversation, I told him that I was not that surprised about what had happened between Lisa and Steve. Several times, I told him, I had smiled at men in various situations; sometimes just being friendly, other times as an indication that I wanted to get to know the guy better and was later stunned that the smile had been interpreted by the man as a sexual invitation.

Malcolm smiled, "I will be careful", he said. I must have looked confused because he explained, "You have been smiling at me a lot."

Your assignment is to respond to this fable in point or short essay form. Try to cover the following issues. It would be ideal to use psychological vocabulary and concepts in responding.

1. What is a main idea of this chapter?

2. The chapter points out that the same specific behavior might mean completely different things to different people. Explain how each of confirmation bias, overconfidence, and belief perseverance might lead each person to believe that their own perception is 'right' and the other 'wrong' and thus impair efforts to bridge the gap between perceptions.

3. What are some steps that men and women can take to minimize the communication confusions that exist between them?

4. (Optional question-only needs to be answered if you feel you can or want to contribute).
Moving away from the specific to a more general theme, do you think that males and females interpret social signals differently?

For example, a woman smiling at a man might intend to be friendly, whereas he might interpret her behavior as a sexual interest. Are there some general ways in which signals are misinterpreted, between the genders? It seems that this might be true particularly with perceptions about 'closeness'. It seems that Lisa was interested in having a social and emotional connection, at least at first, with Steve. He seems to have been interested in having a physical connection first. Signals about the kind of closeness intended were confused.

7.

Emotion

Malcolm was driving me to the University. We were going to visit Elinore there. As we left the house, Malcolm went out the door backwards. I had noticed this curious behavior before. I flagged this behavior in my mind but did not ask about it right away. The drive would take about 30 minutes and we had only gone a few blocks when I could not stop myself from asking him, "Why do you walk through doors backwards?"

He gave a little laugh and shrugged his shoulders, "I see you noticed one of my little rituals."

Silence followed. He was going to make it sound like it was no big deal. I waited a couple of blocks but there was no more explanation, no more information about him. I wanted to know more. "One of them? What else do you do?"

"What harm is there in going through doors backwards? It's just a habit. Don't worry about it."

"I am not worried, I just want to know more about you. I told you a lot about me over dinner. I really know very little about you. I am curious about you," I tried to explain.

"Yes, I tried to understand you as a person, but you are only trying to find out about my rituals just to make fun of me, you probably think I am weird for doing them," he answered in a slightly louder voice. He sat up straighter and tensed his shoulders.

"I don't need to talk about it if it bothers you, Malcolm. My intention was to find out about you, not to criticize you." His angry and defensive reaction took me by surprise and I tried to calm him. I turned my eyes straight ahead and moved as far from him as possible.

He sped up, we were passing cars all of a sudden. Traffic was very heavy. A truck blew its horn as we cut it off. Malcolm's hands gripped the steering wheel tightly. His jaw was tense, brows furrowed. "I resent being made fun of by someone who does not understand me. I really hate it." There was anger in his voice as he sped up to go through a yellow light. I decided that if I wanted to get to the University in one piece, I should be quiet for the rest of the trip. Fifteen tense minutes went by. Gradually we slowed to normal speed and I could see his fingers relax around the steering wheel.

"Look," he finally said quietly, "we are both overreacting."

"I am sorry if I made it sound like I was treating you as though you had something wrong with you, I would like to understand more about you", I wanted to get past his defensiveness without another outburst.

"I might tell you, but I need to check something out with you before I decide," he said this looking at me not the traffic.

"Can we pull over and talk, I want us to be able to concentrate," I wanted to do this safely and I did not want to be in a speeding car if he got upset again.

He found a parking space. He turned the engine off and faced me. "I need your understanding on this Mariah. I have some rituals that I do. They make no sense to other people and some people give me looks like they think I am crazy. I have tried to stop but I have not been successful. So, I accept that I do this. The last thing I need from a friend is judgment. To me, friendship means unconditional support. You must accept me as

I am. Don't even think about changing me. Can I count on you to support me this way?"

Without waiting for an answer, he started driving again. I stayed silent. We had arrived at the University.

We found Elinore sitting in an office. After chatting, we left. This time I drove. I had been thinking about his need for complete and unquestioning support. I was not sure that I could give him that. Shouldn't one help a friend who is doing things that are unreasonable and troublesome? I told Malcolm that I would try to not judge him and that I wanted to hear more.

"I have these rituals. I walk through doors backwards. Recently, I have had to touch certain pages in my textbooks before I start to read. Also, I need to do things in a specific order for example when I am dressing. Left sock, underwear, right sock, and so on. Also, I can't bear to have mushy food touching solid food on my plate. I won't eat it if it's like that."

He looked calmer and more open than before. "Why do you do this?" I asked.

"I have some thoughts that I can't get rid of. These thoughts tell me that something horrible will happen to me or to members of my family if I don't do the rituals. These thoughts never entirely go away. They invade my head all the time, at the most unexpected moments. I have tried to ignore or resist the thoughts but no matter how hard I try, before long they come back stronger than ever."

He looked discouraged. But then he smiled. "On the plus side, my rituals have worked. Nothing terrible has happened, so far."

"Are you implying there is a causal connection between the two things?"

"I don't want to take the chance of finding out. Can you imagine how I would feel if I stopped doing a tiny behavior like the door thing and something awful happened to someone I love?"

I tried to be reasonable. "I could see that if there was any possible connection between you doing rituals and accidents to your family, but I can't see it. Besides, some of these rituals must interfere with your life." I tried to concentrate both on the conversation and the driving.

"Sometimes I worry about that", he acknowledged. "You are right. I worry that the rituals are becoming more time consuming. In my mind, I sometimes worry that I won't have time to do anything other than the rituals. They could take over my whole life."

I tried to articulate the thoughts that were bothering me. "You know what you said about wanting complete and unconditional support? Is that really what good friends do? To me, supporting a friend who is doing senseless and potentially damaging things seems like a coward's way. Let's say you Malcolm, had a friend who was into drugs and developing a dependency, or having a really bad relationship, or anorexic: would you just support them in what they are doing? Or would you try to lead them to better choices?"

I had to slam on the brakes to avoid hitting a car that had stopped in front of us. The conversation was getting heavier than I intended and taking much of my attention.

"You can't stop another person from doing what he wants, its not my job to tell a friend how to live, everyone makes their own choices," he answered.

"I wonder if it is as clear cut as you say. I might not judge someone or tell her how to live, but still feel I have something to contribute that might be useful. I might offer information, a perspective, options that the friend has not thought of. Isn't that what good friends do?"

"No, no matter what, you are not in your friend's shoes, in his head, in his heart. Two people seldom have the same viewpoint", he was getting louder again.

I did not want to let up. "Exactly my point, that's why two heads are better than one at solving problems."

"Perhaps I would agree with you", he said heatedly, "if I didn't think that what you really meant was that your head is better than mine at solving my problems. Really, you must think I am odd or sick for having these rituals."

I could see the tension returning to his jaw. It also bothered me that he was again thinking that my attempts to talk to him about his rituals were motivated by me feeling superior or trying to ridicule him. I thought it best to leave the topic for another time.

Your task is to respond to this in about 350-500 words. If you are motivated to write more that is OK, I will gladly read more, but more is not required. I would like you to consider questions 1-6 in framing your response. You may answer them all briefly, or go into greater depth with just one or two. It is important to demonstrate understanding of the terminology and concepts of the emotion chapter and lectures in your response.

1. What are some possible cognitive aspects to Malcolm's anger?

2. How might the particular situation (driving, being alone with Mariah, to whom he seems attracted) act on his physiology to contribute to his experience of anger?

3. Malcolm seems to express the most anger when Mariah tries to pin him down about his 'rituals'. Do you think that his expression (or display) of anger verbally and with muscle tension helps release the anger, makes no difference, or does it escalate his experience of anger?

4. The most troublesome emotions to most people are anger and jealousy. Do you think we could eliminate these emotions from our lives? Why or why not? Would it be preferable to live without these emotions, if it were possible to do so?

5. Has the chapter in the text given you any ideas on how one might manage their own anger and jealousy?

6. Do you agree with Malcolm that a good friend supports unconditionally? Or with Mariah that a good friend confronts when she believes her friend is on a troublesome path?

8.

Personality

A few days later Elinore were in the car, driving home. She asked me about my relationship with Malcolm.

"I like some things about him", I said. "He is thoughtful and attentive, and he is truly smart. But there are some things about him that really worry me. I am not sure it is a good idea for me to have a close relationship with him."

"What concerns you?" Elinore asked.

"His rituals. He has so many. They are taking over his life. They make no sense, its weird. And he is not doing anything about it. I can understand him having a problem, I can't understand him not dealing with it." I surprised myself by how upset and helpless I felt just talking about it. "Why doesn't he show some willpower and just stop?"

"I am truly glad that you have opened up to me on this, Mariah", she said. "I have been wondering how you two were doing. Would you like to discuss it with me?"

"I respect what your opinion", I replied truthfully. However, there was a part of me that did want to keep some feelings private.

"Look", she started, "I feel you are really struggling with where you want your relationship with Malcolm to go. Is that right?"

"Yes", I admitted reluctantly.

She took one hand off the steering wheel and patted my shoulder. "It is hard to assess ahead of time how a relationship will work. I can see you are thinking about the possibility of a serious relationship with him. Sometimes it's hard to assess the potential of a relationship; how it will be in the long run. Some people don't think very carefully or rationally before becoming emotionally involved. Of course, it's a lot harder to think rationally after you are emotionally attached," she smiled.

"There are many possible approaches to try to figure out how two people will get along with each other", she continued. "You can see if you have mutual interests; you can see if you have mutual goals; you can see if the other person has good personal values and habits. You can see if he is kind, patient, responsible, trusting, a good listener, empathetic, warm, or quick to anger. You can see if communication is deep and workable. You can try to assess the level of commitment."

"Mariah, all of the things are important. However, one approach that has received some validation for being able to predict behavior for the long run is the 'Big Five Trait Theory' of personality. Do you know it?" This conversation was taking an unexpected turn.

"I remember a bit from my psychology courses" I replied cautiously.

"I will review the key points", she said. "We don't all approach life in the same way. We differ in our styles of thinking, our preferences, our behavior, and our emotions. A person's traits are their characteristic ways of thinking, acting, and feeling. These traits appear to be fairly stable over time. Really, when you marry someone you can't expect their traits to change."

"Modern psychology has identified five key traits. People differ from each other along these trait dimensions. A person can be at one or the other extreme end, in terms of each of these traits, or more likely, somewhere nearer the middle.

"The first of the five traits is 'emotional stability'. A person high on this trait is calm, patient and even-tempered", she explained. "A person low on this trait is temperamental, tends to big mood swings, and to worry a lot.

The second trait is 'extraversion'. A person high on this trait is sociable, talkative, and spontaneous. A person low on extraversion is introverted, that is tends to be a quiet, reserved, and controlled person who does not put a priority on interacting with other people.

The third trait is 'openness'. Being high on this trait implies a person who is imaginative, curious, creative, and wanting to try new things. A person low on this trait would likely prefer routine activities, foods, and places.

Fourth is 'agreeableness', a person high on agreeableness tends to be cooperative, sharing, trusting, empathetic and friendly. An individual low on this trait tends to be suspicious, selfish, and antagonistic.

The fifth and last trait, is 'conscientiousness'. A person high on this trait is likely to be hardworking, ambitious, and reliable. Being low on this trait implies a person who tends to be aimless, careless, and undependable."

"As I said, these traits are fundamental to how people experience the world and how they make their way through the world; they tend to be stable over the life span. If you want to project what life with Malcolm might be like, think about him in terms of these traits. If you can figure out where he stands on each of the five, you will get a pretty good idea of his priorities, preferences, and reactions."

She went off. I had nothing pressing so I took out a piece of paper and tried to figure out where Malcolm was on the five traits. With respect to emotional stability, the evidence was clear. He is a huge worrier, as exemplified by his rituals. He is emotionally volatile as demonstrated by his reactions when I tried to question him in the car about the rituals. Rating him on extraversion was easy. He is low on this. He is not outgoing. Openness to experience was a bit harder. I didn't know him well enough to be sure but he is probably average. Aside from the outburst about his rituals, he was amazingly thoughtful and cooperative so he is surely agreeable. He also seemed very conscientious.

At supper, I discussed my impressions of Malcolm with Elinore. "I agree with how you rate him", she said. "Of particular importance is his high score on agreeableness and conscientiousness".

"Look at these last two traits. A partner who is agreeable is likely to share resources. A partner who is conscientious is likely to be dependable and trustworthy. Both traits are likely to enhance survival and quality of life for their partners and children."

I wanted to slow things down. Was Elinore really thinking about how Malcolm and I would function as parents?

"However, before we go further, I want you to think about where you stand on the five traits. Then we can try and figure out how you and Malcolm match up", she said. That answered my unspoken question.

I started to rate myself. I thought I was high on the trait of emotional stability and fairly high on extraversion. On openness, I thought I was in the middle. On the other two traits of agreeableness and conscientiousness we were both high and would rate close to each other.

So, how do the two of us fit together? There are big differences on emotional stability and extraversion; on the other three traits we are quite similar.

Next morning, I asked Elinore. "In a partner, would you suggest that I look for someone who has traits that are similar to mine? Or should I look for someone who has different traits, so we are complementary?"

"That is a brilliant question", she said with excitement. "Recent studies of interpersonal relationships have clarified the importance of trait similarity to satisfaction in relationships. These studies emphasize the beneficial effects of similarity between two partners. They find that partners who begin with similar traits actually become even more like each other over time. Partners who start off relatively more different than similar, undergo a process in which they change away from each other. The trait gaps actually diverge, moving even further apart than they were when they initially got together. Other research confirms that although opposites seem more exciting and appealing for the short term, being with people with similar profiles is more satisfying over the long haul.

She went on to explain in more detail. "When we behave a certain way in the presence of our partner, we expect our partner to react in a way that is accepting of us as an individual. If I am fearful and anxious, I expect my partner to acknowledge those feelings, not to dismiss them. It is easier for a fearful and anxious partner to do so, than for an assertive, confident partner. If I am confident and secure, it is easier for a confident and secure partner to validate those feelings than it is for a fearful one. When my behavior gets a response from my partner that is accepting and validating, then the chances of satisfaction in the relationship are high. The chances for such compatible behaviors are highest when two partners are similar with respect to their traits.

Similarity of traits also encourages reciprocal behavior, which involves responding in kind. If I enjoy meeting new people, trying new food, and traveling it is much easier for a partner who prefers the same things to provide them, than for a partner who is not open in this way. It is also easier for me to provide the things that my partner wants, if I enjoy them. Such reciprocity is another way of validating or accepting another's value as an individual.

"Do you remember the song, 'You don't send me flowers anymore?' The subtext of that lyric is: 'My behavior doesn't elicit from you the validating behaviors it used to.' In a marriage people prefer a context in which they can behave naturally. Introverts want to introvert, extroverts want to extrovert; agreeable people want to agree; anything else is unsatisfying."

I thought about what Elinore had said. I was not sure if I completely agreed with her. I wanted to examine the other point of view. "Sure, similarity can make life smooth. A couple with high trait similarity might never encounter the really tough times that couples who have huge trait differences face as they try and work on the conflicts that are rooted deep within differences in their personalities."

I continued. "Yes, a partner with different traits will make life harder. Each partner will often be frustrated and mystifying to the other. They will have to work extremely hard to understand each other. The gaps will be hard and sometimes appear insurmountable. There will be times when they think the other person is from a different planet."

"If they can get beyond the frustrations, they will have two huge benefits. First, as a team, the couple will have available a broader range of resources for facing the problems that life throws at them. That is instead of two people who are similar to each other and approach things similarly, that is with one reaction, they would have two options for facing what life throws at them. Second, are the advantages for their children. The children will have a more diverse genetic background as far as personality goes. As well, they will have a broader range of parental models. Both factors will make it more likely that the children will be better rounded in terms of personality, rather than being almost like the clone of two parents who are so similar, they might as well be one."

"Hmmm", said Elinore, noncommittally, "this issue will require further thought."

There are some options about how to respond. What is important is that you demonstrate that you understand and have thought about trait theory. You don't have to agree with it. Answer one of the following:

Option 1. You are running a service that attempts to find marriage partners for single people. Malcolm and Mariah have, independently applied (for this example assume they have the personality traits in the story but have not yet met). Based on their traits how would you think this couple might relate to each other if you matched them up? Would they enjoy similar activities? Would they expect similar things from each other? What issues might arise in the relationship? What might be their strengths as a couple? Based on their personality traits, how well do you think they could function as a couple? You can speculate, based at least partly on trait theory. Remember that they differ on emotional stability and extraversion; and are similar on the other three traits.

Option 2. You are still running the marriage service. In a more general sense, how important would you think it is to match people on their trait similarity as opposed to matching on factors such as intelligence, motivations, values, and interests. Explain.

Option 3. Trait theories have to deal with the fact that human behavior may not produce consistent patterns across situations.

For example, you might consider yourself an extroverted person (or have another particular trait). But are you always extroverted? Factors that might influence your extroversion are internal emotional factors (happy, sad, angry, etc); factors about the other persons you are interacting with (stranger, friend, etc); and the situation (how many people present, kind of occasion, etc). Take one of your personality traits and consider how consistent or inconsistent that trait is across situations and over time.

Option 4. How useful do you think trait theory is in understanding and predicting people's behavior?

9.

Fears, Rituals, and Mental Disorders

Who can draw the line in the rainbow where the violet tint ends and the orange tint begins? Distinctly we see the difference of colors, but where exactly does the one first blendingly enter into the other? So with sanity and insanity.
-Herman Melville, Billy Budd

Elinore continued putting a lot of energy into talking to me about my feelings for Malcolm. I liked her attention, and it was good to talk as I was confused about Malcolm. I liked him but his rituals worried and repelled me. I had been thinking about him when Elinore came in to the kitchen.

"When are you going to be seeing Malcolm?" she asked, in what felt to me was a slightly pushy opening question. Her approach put me on the defensive and I reacted more strongly than I intended.

"Thank you for the information you gave me on personality traits. You were most helpful. I have thought it over and I came to the conclusion that the trait differences between Malcolm and I would make for some relationship struggles but they are not an insurmountable problem. But something else is."

"I just can't see myself committing to a man who is", I hesitated how to continue because I knew she liked Malcolm, but decided to let it out, "not normal. I think he displays obsessive-compulsive disorder. He has these obsessive thoughts that some dire consequence is going to happen to his family or friends if he does not engage in the compulsive rituals. He can't get rid of the thoughts. I don't think he really tries very hard to put them out of his mind. His rituals are increasing. It's sad. He could be such a great guy. Its scary to see someone you like, act in such an irrational and bizarre way. I feel so utterly helpless when I see him doing those rituals."

"So Mariah, let me see if I understand. You like him, but you are uncertain whether Malcolm can ever overcome his rituals. They could get worse and interfere more with his life. You are unable to understand his behavior and are therefore scared and helpless in the face of it. You are so repelled that you are ready to identify and label Malcolm as having a mental disorder. Is that correct?"

I didn't like the way she twisted the subject away from Malcolm's actions onto my judgments. All of a sudden I felt I was the one being scrutinized, instead of Malcolm's behavior. I had to defend myself. "Well, you can't tell me you think its normal to spend about two hours each day doing compulsive rituals. To be so out of control, that you won't stop? To refuse to discuss it. To get angry, when a friend tries to help? Do you think he is a poster boy for mental health?" My voice had risen in volume. I realized that I was frustrated and sarcastic. Fleetingly, I wondered what the source of my frustration was. Did it come from Elinor, or Malcolm, or was it with myself for not being able to get a better handle on what was going on? I did not stay with this thought because Elinor continued with a different approach.

"Mariah, its important to remember that we all live in a world that has some uncertainty. We can't predict and control everything about our lives and the lives of people close to us. Uncertainty and a partially uncontrollable and unpredictable future remain an inescapable feature of human existence. I don't want to think about it, but I know it."

I understood what she was saying but I was not sure how this 'uncertainty' and 'unpredictability' related to Malcolm.

"When people are under stress, they do things that are silly. I read my horoscope, I wear my 'lucky' ring, and I 'knock on wood'. Mariah, you know me. I am an intelligent, rational person. I know that the horoscope is composed of statements that sound informative but actually can be applied to practically anyone at anytime. I know that the ring I wear can't possibly affect my future. I rationally know these things. Yet, I found comfort in these superstitions or rituals. They gave me the illusion that I could control the uncontrollable. Why is it so bad that Malcolm has a few more of these behaviors than I do?"

"I can't believe that you are placing Malcolm's obsessive-compulsive rituals and your tiny superstitions in the same context", I protested. "His are weird, his are time consuming, his could interfere with his life, his are painful for me to watch. Your superstitions are pretty ordinary", I finished.

"There is one more big difference", Elinor said quietly, "he suffers with his." I sat quietly as her words sank in. I had always known Malcolm suffered even though he sometimes pretended that he didn't. In fact, last time he and I talked he had said something about wanting to overcome his rituals, but just not knowing where to start. I had ignored the comment at the time, but now I mentioned it to Elinor.

"Do you think that was his way of asking for your help?" she inquired. "If it was, that is huge, he has opened the door. In fact, I would think there is a responsibility for his friends to help out as best as they can."

"How do you think people start on these rituals?" I asked.

"There are so many ways to develop superstitious beliefs that I sometimes wonder how anyone escapes these forces," she started. "It must start in childhood. Do you know how many magical and superstitious beliefs we teach our children? Four-leaf clovers and luck, magic objects such as stones, making a wish while throwing coins in fountains, blowing out candles on a birthday cake, fairy tales, songs and so on; all these encourage children to think magically rather than rationally. We encourage them to believe in Santa Claus and to put out milk and cookies for him and his reindeer. Can you think of a better way to encourage magical thinking in children?

"When people get older, peers become increasingly important. Many superstitions come with membership in a group. Sports teams develop rituals that are supposed to bring luck. Teen groups develop their own rituals that may involve candles, songs, or pretended occult actions. They serve to create a bonded group of insiders against the rest of the world. Many adolescents are fascinated with magic. It fits in with the common idea at that age that they are special in some way. Believing in magic is a way of rising above the mundane. Often membership in an adolescent peer group socializes an individual to these beliefs.

"Superstitions can also arise in a completely different way. Consider the student who wears a certain green sweater to an exam that she is worried about. She has prepared but she is still anxious. She does very well on the exam. The sweater can acquire magical powers because it has been paired with a significant successful event. Or, the person is fearing some event such as an accident or illness, engages in some rituals and the dreaded event does not occur. The person makes the connection between the rituals and avoidance of the event. As you can see this is accidental conditioning at work.

"Once conditioning and socialization have established a ritual or superstition, then the way our minds work tends to maintain these habits. We are all subject to confirmation bias. You remember Mariah, that's our powerful tendency to notice, remember, and give significance to instances that confirm what we already believe, in this case that rituals work, and to ignore, forget, dismiss, or explain away the instances where they do not work. So our student in the green sweater is likely to think, 'I passed because I wore the sweater'. If she does not pass, she is likely to think that she did not study hard enough, or to just forget about that particular instance. Likely she will not associate the failure to the sweater.

I was getting intrigued. Maybe Malcolm was not as irrational as I had thought. There might be an explanation for his behavior. "So what can be done about this kind of problem?" I asked.

"The first thing you want to keep in mind is that his rituals are a way of maintaining the illusion that he can have control over what happens to other people such as his family and friends. The uncertainty of aspects of life scares him. He is anxious. He is not coping with his anxiety in an effective way."

"Remember that people with anxiety disorders frequently feel isolated and alone. This is particularly true for individuals who have superstitious rituals. They are often ashamed of or confused by the unusual nature of their symptoms and are understandably hesitant to discuss their problem with others. Often they actively hide their symptoms from others."

"So its easy for a vicious cycle to develop. The sufferer engages in the rituals, feels bad and isolated, this leads to increased anxiety, more rituals to cope with the increased anxiety, greater isolation and negative thoughts, and so on. Sometimes I think it really does not matter what started it. The origin is irrelevant. The vicious cycle is what is important. You need to help Malcolm learn to replace that with a healthy upward spiral."

"How can I help him do I do that?" I asked.

"Well, first thing is that you don't do anything that is going to increase his anxiety, such as attacking his behavior and putting him on the defensive. That would just make things worse." I bit my lip as I remembered how I had handled it the first time it came up.

"Secondly, you need to give him some hope. He sees no way out. If he stops the rituals, he believes disaster would strike. He cares about others and does not want to take that chance. You need to guide him to a way out of this terrible dilemma.

"Third, you need to help him think rationally about his behavior. It might be difficult for him to do that as long as he is highly anxious. But you need to work on it. See, Malcolm needs to move toward the point that he comes to realize that he is completely trapped by his thinking. Do you know what I mean by trapped?"

"Yes, I think so. As long as he believes what he now believes he can't stop the rituals. His thinking has to change for any improvement to occur", I answered. "He has a hypothesis in his mind. The hypothesis is: 'If I stop the rituals, then a disaster will happen'. He doesn't want to take the risk, yet as long as he maintains the rituals, the hypothesis remains unfalsifiable."

"I am confused", I continued. "I took what you said about his anxiety to mean that I should be gentle with him. Now you are suggesting that I need to work on changing his thoughts. That can't be easy or gentle for him."

"Be easy on his emotions, be firmer with his thinking errors", Elinore advised. "Point out the unfalsifiablity. Point out that in the real world, his rituals can't possibly affect the welfare of others in a positive way. If anything, their effect would be negative. He is wasting time and energy in his rituals that could be better directed toward the welfare of his family and friends." We lapsed into quiet thought. After a while, I began to see a way.

With excitement I said, "How about if I can get him to give up one tiny part, just one minor little detail, of his ritual for one day? Probably no significantly evil event would befall his family or friends that day", I continued. "Possibly that would be a demonstration to him that there is no link between his rituals and avoidance of disaster."

Elinore thought quietly. Then she became animated. "Brilliant, I love it", she enthused. "Taking a small step such as what you suggest could be the first of many bigger steps toward limiting his rituals. What I really love about it is that you are using the empirical method to challenge his beliefs. If he stops one tiny part of one ritual for one day and no disaster happens, it will demonstrate to him that the link he believed in does not exist. If he can see that for himself, it will be more powerful than someone trying to persuade him."

"I would hope that once he sees this, he would be able to have the curiosity and the interest to experiment with giving up a bit more of his rituals. One small step could possibly get him off his present downward cycle and to start him on a positive spiral of hope and reason!" she continued."

"Surely, that would not be enough by itself", I said more cautiously.

Eventually, we had a more complete plan. First, I would ask Malcolm if he wanted our support. If he said he did, I would explain to him how Elinore and I believed his thoughts had been hijacked by anxiety, fear, and unfalsifiability. I would suggest that he drop one tiny part of one ritual. He would choose exactly what and when and how.

At the same time, we would encourage Malcolm to develop more effective coping skills. These could include reducing stress by becoming more physically active; working on channeling his thoughts to more positive areas; and dealing with worries in practical ways.

You can respond to this in 350 words (or more). Based on the text (and also your own thoughts).

Option 1. Do you think Malcolm has a 'mental condition'? Answer in terms of the text's definitions. Are there any advantages or disadvantages to defining, or relating to his behavior, as a psychological disorder? Are there any advantages/disadvantages to relating to his behavior as a minor extension of the kind of perfectly usual and normal superstition that many, maybe most if not all, people practice? What are the consequences of thinking of him as having a psychological disorder?

Option 2. This story highlights the potential importance of an individual's thoughts to mood and to mental health. We have come across the idea that anorexic women believe that they look heavier than they actually are; and that this thought is a significant part of their condition. We have discussed the idea that depressed people interpret information about themselves in a more negative way than non-depressed individuals. People who interpret difficult situations as a challenge, rather than as a threat, experience less stress. In all these instances, as with Malcolm, the thought is important.

So think of a character from fiction, movies, or from your personal experience in terms of these ideas and analyze the thought and its consequences. For example: Joan of Arc, Angelina Jolie character in "Girl Interrupted", Jack Nicholson character in "As Good as It Gets". Whatever topic you choose for this option draw specific links between the character's cognitions (thoughts, beliefs, interpretations) and the mood and/or psychological illness.

10.

Attributions

I had phoned Malcolm and told him that Elinore and I had discussed a plan to help him gain more control over the rituals. He and I met for coffee. I could tell that he was anxious about the topic but he had agreed to meet. I was a little worried about how our talk would go. I cared about Malcolm and wanted to help. I sensed he was open to me yet the topic was delicate and I did not want to make him anxious or offend him.

I got straight into it. "Malcolm, I have been thinking about your rituals in terms of attribution theory. Attribution theory is about how people explain the cause of behavior. For example, a person does badly on a test and thinks 'the teacher is disorganized, the textbook is unclear, the test unfair'. In his mind, what caused the poor mark? Events outside him, external things. This is one kind of attribution; finding the cause of behavior outside the person."

"Lets say a few weeks later the same individual obtains a great mark on a test. In his mind what caused this? His brilliance, his hard work, his ability to figure out what would be on the test. This is the other kind of attribution; the behavior is caused by things internal to the person, that is his or her disposition (nature, personality)."

"Let me make sure if I got it right", he said. "Suppose I am late for a class. If the professor thinks I am lazy and unmotivated, he makes an internal, dispositional, attribution about me, about the reason for my lateness. Or he can think, the traffic was bad; which would be a situational or external attribution about why I am late."

"Perfect example", I responded. "And of course the professor's attitude to you will be greatly influenced by the attribution he is making. In this case if he thinks the cause is external he will be sympathetic to you. If he thinks the cause is internal to you, he will be less sympathetic. Another example: suppose someone, perhaps your partner, behaves in a hostile and angry way. You can attribute the behavior to the situation that the person is in, maybe a bad day at work; or to their disposition, the person is by nature a hostile and angry individual. Makes quite a difference in how you will react!"

I continued with the main thread. "So we (and others) do things, we behave. Then we ask 'why? Why did I, or he, she, or they do that?' In answer we provide either an internal (dispositional) or external (situational) attribution.

Malcolm nodded to signify he understood. He had such kind and intelligent eyes. I got into the more personal side. "I tried to analyze your rituals in terms of attribution theory. It was confusing. You believe that you can avoid bad things happening by continuing to engage in rituals. I first thought that because you think you can control bad things by your behavior, you were making a dispositional attribution. But when I thought about it more, I came to the opposite conclusion. I asked myself, 'why does Malcolm do the rituals?' My answer was, 'to avoid bad things happening to him or to people close to him'. When I look at it this way, it becomes clear that you attribute your behavior to an external cause, namely the bad things which you are trying to avoid."

"So what difference does that make if the attribution I make about my behavior is dispositional or situational?" he asked.

"Well", I started cautiously, "there are some potential problems with attributing to situational cause. If you believe the ritualistic behavior is under external control then you implicitly believe that your won't be able to control it. That can't be a positive feeling."

"OK, I can see that. But I don't see how I am any further ahead."

"Let me explain more. Obviously we feel much more effective when we attribute an internal cause to our behaviors", I replied.

"Interesting, but what does it have to do with me?" he asked.

"Elinore and I came up with the idea that you may want to explore how you can gradually gain control over your rituals. Once you achieve that, you will be able to make the attribution that you are in control of your behavior, not some external situation. Wouldn't you just feel better?"

He looked curious but skeptical. "How could I do this?"

I explained the idea of stopping one tiny part of his ritual for one day, as a start. I told him that when nothing seriously bad happens to him or his family that day, it will demonstrate that the link he perceives between rituals and avoidance of bad things does not exist. I appealed to his intelligence and to his belief in the scientific method. If a decrease in ritual behavior did not lead to an increase in bad things happening that would suggest there is no link between the two things. It was a logical procedure that I hoped that he would not resist. I could see that he was thinking it over. But then to my disappointment, he suddenly shook his head.

"Thanks for trying to help. But I can't do it. I would just get too worried. I would fear that something bad would happen and would feel guilty that I did not do everything I could to avoid it. I guess I am just a worrier. That's the way I am. I can't see myself stopping the rituals and becoming a laid back, relaxed, easy-going kind of guy."

I was becoming frustrated. "Malcolm, look at what you have just done. You have made a bunch of attributions. You have said you are a worrier and you will always be that way."

"Hey, but at least they are internal, dispositional attributions. You said that internal attributions are better than external ones, didn't you?" I couldn't tell whether he was arguing just to be difficult or whether I had been unclear. I realized I had oversimplified the idea about internal attributions being good and external ones being unhelpful.

"You are right", I acknowledged. "I wasn't precise enough before. It's definitely good to make internal attributions about your abilities, strengths, and successes. While you want to give credit to other people or situations that help you, you also want to give credit to yourself. But it's not as good to make internal attributions about your failures, or even your potential failures, as you are doing right now. It's especially unhelpful to make negative internal attributions if these attributions are incorrect."

I realized that I should be precise. "Malcolm, I don't mean that you should blame situations for all your shortcomings. But it definitely makes no sense to make attributions to the effect that you are helpless and will always be that way. Not only are you making internal attributions about your present inability to change, you are saying you will never change. How can you possibly know that you can't change now or in the future?"

"Because that's the way it is. I will always be a loser."

I felt ready to give up. I didn't want to get mad. I tried a slightly different approach. "Malcolm, is anything that I have said about attributions resonating with you?"

"Mariah, you are just trying to prove some theory. Why are you picking on me? Am I just a great subject for your experiment? I bet this whole thing is about you demonstrating just how clever you can be, how you can control me."

My frustration boiled over. "Malcolm you are still doing it. Now you are making negative dispositional attributions about me. You just implied I am trying to help you because of some personal need I have. How do you think that makes both of us feel? Is it not possible that I am trying to be helpful? Wouldn't it be nice if you could actually make some positive attributions about both of us." I was nearly losing control.

"You know what would be really nice", he said angrily, "is if you started talking like my girlfriend instead of like a walking textbook." With that he left, just walked out without another word. I tried to attribute his behavior to his anxiety about the rituals, not to anything that I had done.

That evening he dropped by without calling. He was wringing his hands, standing awkwardly at the door. I invited him in. He was apologetic.

"I have had a chance to think about what you said. You know, I just feel so helpless about the rituals. And I get even more anxious when I am questioned about them. I feel attacked and have a panicky reaction. I am sorry I lashed out at you." He looked down at the floor.

I felt sorry for him. "I didn't like the way you treated me. But I do understand your feelings. Lets move on."

"I agree. I would like you to tell me more about the plan. What do you think should be the first step?"

"I think you should pick a small ritual to give up for a day, something that won't cause too much anxiety."

"What exactly do you suggest?" he asked.

I wanted him to have control. "It might be a good idea for you to pick the ritual. Something small."

He decided to first work on the ritual that he had about having to go through doors backwards. It was a ritual that took a lot of maneuvering to manage, especially in trying to make it look natural. He was afraid that others, beside me, would notice. He decided that at least a couple of times a day, starting tomorrow he would walk through doors normally. I encouraged that as a good start. I suggested that later he could follow-up by dropping other rituals step-by-step, with some guidance and at a pace that would not make him overly anxious.

He left, looking positive.

A few days later, he came in happily. Most of the time he had been walking through doors normally. Nothing tragic had happened to him or his family.

He told me that he hoped that taking this small step would be the first of many bigger steps toward limiting his rituals. He talked openly about how his thoughts had been hijacked by anxiety, fear, and unfalsifiability. He was determined to work toward improvement.

He thanked me. "I owe this progress to you Mariah. Without you I would have no hope." He gave me a big hug.

As we let go of each other, I felt compelled to say. "I appreciate your acknowledgement. But I must point out that you still need to watch your attributions!

"I know, I know, he said, I acknowledge your help but I recognize that I also contributed to my progress."

I smiled, "great attributions."

Respond by showing that you understand attributions and their consequences.

One way to do this would be to think of an instance when you made an attribution about yourself.

Think about the attribution. Was it dispositional or situational? If it was dispositional was it about a limited aspect of the you or was it global? (did the attribution refer to a disposition that would emerge only in limited circumstances or to a disposition that would influence your behavior much of the time).

What were the consequences of the attribution? (did it make you feel positive, or in control; or did the attribution act to limit your perception of your potential; did it make you blame yourself or others; was credit given accurately or not?) Was the original attribution made on limited information? Did subsequent information change the attribution or did it 'stick' regardless of subsequent events?

Alternatively, you can think of an example when someone made an attribution you; or you made an attribution about someone else. Explore these ideas.

References and Further Reading

Introduction and Chapter 1

Adler, M. (1991). Critical thinking programs: why they won't work. http://radicalacademy.com/adlercriticalthinkingpro.htm. Accessed September 10, 2001

Frazier, K (Ed.). (1991) *The hundredth monkey and other paradigms of the paranormal*. New York: Prometheus Books.

Gallup Organization. (2001) Gallup poll analyses: American's belief in psychic and paranormal phenomena is up over the last decade. http://www.gallup.com/search/results.asp Accessed September 10, 2001

Gilovitch, T. (1991) *How we know what isn't so; the fallibility of human reason in everyday life.* New York: The Free Press

Hanonen, J. (Ed.). *Teaching critical thinking in psychology.* Milwaukee: Alverno College

Levy, D.A. (1997) *Tools of critical thinking*. Boston: Allyn & Bacon

Marton, J. (2002) Using specifically written fables to teach critical thinking in introductory psychology. Presented at the annual convention of the Canadian Psychology Association, Vancouver Canada, June 2002.

Peterson, G. (2001). Referred to in the June 8, 2001 summaries at the PESTS (Psychologists educating students to think skeptically) website: http://www.sc.mariposa.edu/sbscience/pests/summaries/010608.html Accessed September 10, 2001

PESTS main site: http://www.sc/mariposa.edu/sbscience/pests

Piatelli-Palmarini, M. (1994). *Inevitable illusions: How mistakes of reason rule our minds.* New York: Wiley & Sons.

Shermer, M. (2002) *Why people believe in weird things; pseudoscience, superstition, and other confusions of our time.* New York: Henry Holt

Stanovich, K.E. (2001). *How To Think Straight About Psychology* (6e). Boston: Allyn & Bacon.

Vyse, S.A (1997). *Believing in Magic; the Psychology of Superstition.* New York: Oxford University Press.

Chapter 3

Caplan, P. J. & Caplan, J. B. (1999). *Thinking Critically About Research on Sex and Gender.* New York: Addison Wesley.

Edmunds, E.M., Cahoon, D., Steed, J.H., & Gardner, W.R. (1995). Social-sexual opinions as a function of gender, self-esteem and menstrual cycle phase. *Psychology: a Journal of Human Behavior,* 32, 22-26.

McFarlane, Jessica; Martin, Carol Lynn; & Williams, Tannis, M. (1988). Mood fluctuations: Women versus men and menstrual versus other cycles. *Psychology of Women Quarterly,* 12, 201-223.

Parlee, Mary Brown (1982). Changes in mood and activation levels during the menstrual cycle in experimentally naïve subjects. *Psychology of Women Quarterly,* 7, 119-131.

Chapter 5

Schacter, D.L. (2001). *The Seven Sins of Memory.* New York: Houghton Mifflin.

ISBN 141203647-X